The Definitive Guide to Marketing Planning

The fast track to intelligent marketing planning and implementation for executives

ANGELA HATTON

 Prentice Hall
FINANCIAL TIMES

An imprint of **Pearson Education**

London · New York · San Francisco · Toronto · Sydney
Tokyo · Singapore · Hong Kong · Cape Town · Madrid
Paris · Milan · Munich · Amsterdam

Pearson Education Limited

Edinburgh Gate
Harlow CM20 2JE
Tel: +44 (0)1279 623623
Fax: +44 (0)1279 431059
Website: www.pearsoned.co.uk

First published in Great Britain in 1996
under the title *Marketing Plans with a winning edge*
This edition published 2000

© Pearson Education Limited 2000

The right of Angela Hatton to be identified as author
of this work has been asserted by her in accordance
with the Copyright, Designs and Patents Act 1988.

ISBN 978-0-273-64932-8

British Library Cataloguing in Publication Data
A CIP catalogue record for this book can be obtained from the British Library

Typeset by Pantek Arts, Maidstone, Kent
Printed and bound in Great Britain by Bell & Bain Ltd, Glasgow

The Publishers' policy is to use paper manufactured from sustainable forests.

Transferred to digital print on demand, 2009
Printed and bound in Great Britain by CPI Antony Rowe, Chippenham and Eastbourne

About the author

Known for her enthusiastic style as a trainer and pragmatism as a consultant, Angela Hatton has worked with organizations large and small across both public and private sectors (including the BBC, IBM, Cable & Wireless, Halifax plc, Lloyds/TSB and Skillset – the National Training Organisation for Film, TV, Video and Multimedia).

Unusually Angela combines an active interest in the academic development of marketing with the practical challenges of implementing strategies, plans and customer orientation in the corporate environment. With over 12 years' experience as an examiner and academic adviser to the Chartered Institute of Marketing, Angela is a visiting lecturer with City University Business School and has her own company, Tactics, which provides tutorial support and distance learning provision for students studying for their marketing qualifications with CIM. You can find out more about Angela and the services provided by Tactics on their website, http://www.tacticsforbusinesssuccess.co.uk

Educated at Fleetwood Grammar School, a degree in Economics from Liverpool University was followed by a Post Graduate Diploma in Hotel Catering and Tourism Management from Surrey University.

Angela Hatton is the author of several publications and for 10 years has written and edited *Marketing Success*, the CIM's quarterly student publication.

To Mandy whose support, energy and sense of humour have made sure Tactics has become expert at getting *more from less*.

To my much loved husband Dave and my friends in the Friday Club who have provided sympathy, support, good wine and good company, reliably and regularly – it's been much appreciated.

Contents

Introduction viii

1   More from less 1
The rationale for marketing planning 2
The manager's role 3
Why marketing? 6
Understanding how the customer focus was lost
    and found again 7
The implications of change 17
A storm of initiatives? 20
Introducing a customer-oriented culture 21
A planning review 26

2   Unravelling the planning puzzle 29
Establishing a planning sequence 30
The problem with plans and planning 30
The hierarchy of plans 31
A planning sequence 34
Reviewing the planning sequence 47
How long does it take? 47
Planning as an activity 51
A planning challenge 53

3   Informing the planners 55
Managing the information input 56
The value of information 56
Data or information 58
The marketing information system 59
Managing marketing research 63

Contents

4 Measuring current market performance 71
Auditing the marketing activity 72
What constitutes the marketing activity? 73
The marketing outputs 75
Portfolio analysis 76
Customer analysis 90
Analyzing performance 102
Summary 106

5 Ensuring the external focus 109
The role of the environmental audit 110
The significance of environmental monitoring 110
Gathering environment intelligence 111
Environmental factors 112
About the competition 116
Contingency and scenario plans 122
Using the environmental audit 123

6 Where are we going? 131
Raising the corporate umbrella 132
The corporate mission and vision 132
Corporate or business objectives 135
Completing the planning gap 137
Filling the planning gap 140
Communicating the strategy 144

7 Implementing corporate strategy 147
Developing the market strategy 148
Components of a marketing plan 149
The marketing background 149
Integrating the marketing mix 165

8   Planning for the 7Ps 169

The tactics of the marketing mix 170
Why do customers buy? 171
Price 179
Promotion 187
Place 188
The extended service mix 189
People 190
Physical evidence 191
Processes 192
Action 192

9   Effective communication 201

A guide to promotional planning 202
Marketers – the messengers 203
The communication process 204
Using the communication tools 211
The communication tools examined 212
The promotional plan 222

10   Implementation and control 227

Making plans work 228
Winning support 229
Motivating the implementers 235
What is internal marketing? 236
Controlling plans 244
Monitoring performance 252
The budget 255
Closing the loop 257

Index 259

Introduction

You may have your own business, or be a captain of industry. You might be trying to juggle priorities in a resource-starved public sector organization or satisfy the needs of a diverse and demanding range of stakeholders. Whether you are a supervisor or managing director your goals will be the same, you will be trying to get the maximum value of outputs from the scarce inputs available to you. You will be striving to get more from less.

The key to your success lies in planning, but the first barrier to that planning is finding the time to plan. Managers frequently have too much to do and seemingly not enough time to do it in. The planning cycle, if it exists formally, is simply another unwelcome task to be undertaken routinely and with little enthusiasm.

Once completed, that plan – often a well presented document – simply gathers dust on the shelf until, spurred on by the need to produce next year's programme, it is revisited. It is dusted off, reviewed and modified to meet the next deadline in a sterile planning process.

In organizations large and small across the business sectors planning activities are:

- top down, so are never owned by those who must implement them
- driven by the priorities of the products or the business rather than the customers. As a result resources may be used efficiently, but the outputs will not offer their maximum potential value in the marketplace – activities are ineffective

- focused on the production of a document rather than the action plan which will direct the operation's activities for the next year
- inflexible – once written they are converted to tablets of stone and cannot be modified irrespective of changing events or market conditions. Such a lack of realism makes the plans little more than useless and ensures middle managers producing plans will always opt for the least risk – the lowest common denominator
- too often produced in isolation from the business plan and not communicated to those charged with its implementation; the marketing planners failing to share the marketing strategy with those developing the communication plan
- too seldom 'sold' to colleagues and the staff who will be responsible for achieving the objectives set
- left to staff who have no real understanding of the tools and frameworks which make the planning process a dynamic and invaluable core of the manager's role.

In this book I have tried to provide an easy to follow guide to the planning process. Its step-by-step approach provides a blueprint for the production of an integrated customer-facing business and marketing plan. The tools of management are surprisingly flexible, they can be adapted and used in a variety of situations and circumstances. Like any craft your competence and confidence with these tools will develop with practice. The planning frameworks provide a methodology which gives logical structure to the process and from which you can evolve a personal style and timetable to suit your needs and those of your organization.

There are many more academic books which provide greater detail of the various tools and in-depth analysis of their value. This book attempts to provide a pragmatic overview of an approach I use when tackling a new consultancy challenge or an academic case study. From this framework you will be able to adapt, modify and develop your own tools and approach. I hope its straightforward approach provides you with a useful insight and overview of customer-oriented planning.

Managers who learn the benefits of planning find that they are more often in control, events less frequently take them by surprise and there is less fire fighting. Staff who know what is happening and what is expected are better able and motivated to forecast and prevent problems. The net result is efficient and effective use of your resources, an output valued by your customers and generating benefits expected by the stakeholders. A recipe for getting more from less.

Key to symbols used

 Tricks of the trade

 Watch out!

 Fast track

 Don't forget

 Example

CHAPTER 1

More from less

The rationale for marketing planning

The manager's role

Why marketing?

Understanding how the customer focus was lost and found again

The implications of change

A storm of initiatives?

Introducing a customer-oriented culture

A planning review

The rationale for marketing planning

Irrespective of your experience as a business planner, you will be no stranger to planning. You already understand the rationale for it, are skilled in the techniques of planning and have a wide variety of planning experiences to draw upon. You will have planned journeys, dinner parties and holidays. You will have used the lessons of time management when juggling a crowded diary and the rules of financial planning whilst trying to stretch an over-extended budget. Besides planning your career, family and possibly your retirement you have probably passed some of your time at work involved with planning. From sales calls to projects and promotional campaigns, all aspects of business activity can benefit from a plan.

The common factor that prompts the production of all these plans is the scarcity of resources. Planning is a method, a basic life skill employed to help us tackle the conundrum of having too much to do and too little to do it with. The planner's toolbox includes techniques for prioritization and decision-making as well as objective-setting and control. All this works towards ensuring that our limited resources are used *efficiently* – that we get the most from every hour and penny spent.

But in the intensely competitive environment of business today, being efficient is simply not enough. In the marketplace of the new millennium customers are as scarce as time or money, and success can only be certain when planning is focused on delivering satisfaction to those precious customers and clients. *Effective* use of scarce resources is as critical as efficient use and is the challenge now faced by the business manager. Marketing planning provides the framework or blueprint for customer-oriented strategies, ensuring business success. It requires time and effort, but the results make that investment worthwhile. The concepts are simple and universally applicable. The managing director of the multinational and the self-employed trader can benefit equally from the disciplines of customer focused planning. The outcomes of the plan are not limited to profit and sales either; the religious leader wishing to increase a congregation, the charity worker hoping to increase donations and the public service administrator will all find marketing planning will help them to get *more from less*.

In this first chapter we will:

- examine in more detail the manager's role in planning
- consider the reasons behind the growing importance of the focus on both customers and quality
- set this recent development in the context of past approaches and styles of management
- consider the implications of customer-oriented planning on culture and organizational structure
- review your own operation's approach to planning and your position in marketing planning.

The manager's role

An organization, whatever its size or constitution, is simply a collection of resources and stakeholders. These might include a workforce contributing its labour, shareholders or partners who have offered financial resources, as well as buildings, equipment and raw materials. Whatever is on the resources inventory, the operation will not be productive without organization. The central activity of the manager involves these resources. He or she is responsible for them and answerable to the stakeholders who contributed them. Stakeholders include anyone with an interest in the activities of the operation, from bank managers and shareholders to employees and suppliers.

Resources are limited and have a value, but the manager is not simply a security guard for them. Keeping them as they are is not adequate; it is only when combined efficiently and effectively that any collection of resources becomes transformed into value-added outputs – see Fig. 1.1.

The process of transformation means that the outputs are worth more than the sum of the costs of the scarce inputs – value has been added. The manager is charged with planning and controlling this transformation process to ensure that resources are employed productively and the value added is maximized.

There are two ways in which the process might be unsuccessful:

- If the scarce resources are wasted, i.e. not used efficiently, then inputs may cost more than the outputs generated.
- If the outputs are not bought, i.e. find no demand, or attract a price too low to cover costs, they will have limited value in the marketplace and so again the transformation process will have been unproductive.

The costs of the inputs must be managed below the value of the outputs if a benefit or profit is to be available for the stakeholders to share.

Fig 1.1 The transformation process

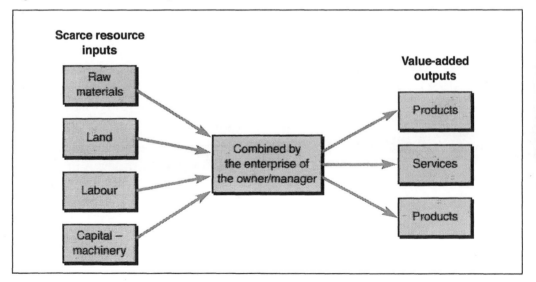

The manager's prime task is to make decisions on how best to employ the organization's resources (planning)

> **'If you're not adding value, get out.'** Tom Peters

and what they should be used to produce to ensure the organization offers the most value/benefits to its customers (marketing) – see Fig. 1.2.

> ★
> - Marketing planning is central to the success of any organization and should be a core competence for all managers.
> - Only if managers can combine the skills and techniques of the planner with the customer-oriented vision of a marketing culture will any organization have a chance of survival, let alone success.

It is important to recognize that we are not treating marketing as an element of the business, i.e. a function of it, but as the driving force and focus for the whole business plan. As

Fig 1.2 How resources are combined

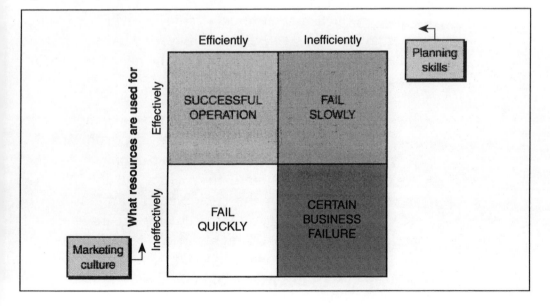

such it is the business planners who must appreciate the concept of marketing and have the skills to implement a customer-oriented approach to all their decisions and business activities.

Why marketing?

Business success has not always been dependent on a customer focus. A review of business and management thinking shows that the critical need to ensure customer satisfaction is a relatively recent dimension of modern business thinking, and even now it is not universally accepted or understood. The role of marketing is still evolving in many companies.

However, others would claim that far from being new to business, marketing is perhaps the oldest business discipline. Certainly no product has ever had any value until a customer could be found for it. The 18th-century economist Adam Smith wrote in *The Wealth of Nations* that the sole purpose of production was consumption. Even then the importance of customers was clearly apparent.

Making products that customers value and will buy is a fundamental business activity, but two developments have changed the emphasis and increased the need for customer champions in any organization:

- Increased competition means customers have more choice and will naturally choose the supplier whose offering they perceive promises them the most satisfaction.
- As organizations expand, they often fall into the trap of losing touch with the customer. Separated both by geography and company hierarchy the business planner makes decisions based on what he or she thinks the customer needs and wants. Decisions are made with the best intentions but by people who are remote from the

customers, who have in turn changed and whose needs are constantly evolving and developing.

No one in any organization, public or private, large or small, should be so arrogant as to make the mistake of thinking that he or she knows what the customer wants. That person will almost certainly be wrong and so cause scarce resources to be wasted producing features and benefits not valued by the customer. There is only one expert when it comes to customer needs – the customer.

Smaller companies, possibly those typical of industry before the mid-20th century, were much closer emotionally and physically to the customer, so the need for formalized customer representation was less obvious. Business decisions perhaps could be seen to reflect naturally customer priorities, and so marketing was an integral element of all managers' thinking. Sadly, distance and corporate growth has rendered that to be a traditional skill almost lost from the craft of management. Today, like a rare species, marketing must be imported, and its growth and spread managed.

The marketing professional is the customer's representative in the organization, the evangelist of the customer's cause. Slowly, as companies rediscover the logic of concentrating their activities on satisfying customers, so the strategic responsibility of the marketing manager will be shared more widely across the management team.

Understanding how the customer focus was lost and found again

Business is and always was an exchange process. Resource inputs exchange for rent, wages, interest and profits. Resource outputs exchange for a price. For any exchange to take place both parties must benefit, i.e. get something out of the deal, or it is not worth transacting. Economists talk of mutually profitable exchange. However, both parties do *not* have to get equal benefit from the exchange. Who gets what depends on the balance of power. In markets the balance of demand and supply determines the relative power between customers and suppliers.

Product orientation

Consider the situation of a *seller's market*: goods are in short supply and there are queues of unsatisfied customers. As a business manager wanting to increase profits, ask yourself how you would behave in this situation.

There are two broad strategies open to you:

- You can raise your prices to ration the available supply and increase your profits.
- You can concentrate on trying to make more goods with your available resources (more from less). Increased output will yield more sales and profit.

You may pursue a combination of these, and collectively firms within industries inevitably do this.

Many economies are still at a stage of economic growth characterized by a seller's market, with power in the hands of the suppliers. In the UK rationing existed until the early 1950s and so there are still managers employed today who began their careers in such marketplaces. Elsewhere, growing economies in the developing world and the newly emerging market economies of Eastern Europe also display the characteristics of a seller's market.

In such a scenario the fact that a customer might prefer the product in a different colour or size, delivered to home or with a flexible finance package is not relevant. The customer has one choice – take it or leave it. There is no incentive for the supplier to worry about a less than satisfied customer because there are plenty more in the queue and he or she can sell as many products as can be made. In the USA this era in their development was enshrined by the often quoted statement of Henry Ford – they can have any colour they want, as long as it's black.

The effort and energy of these managers is understandably inward looking – reviewing the operation to seek ways of increasing efficiency. This culture or philosophy of management is referred to as product/operational orienta-

tion. Management's attention is focused on what is made and how it is made, and the needs of the business and the staff dominate decision-making.

Sales orientation

Markets are not, however, static. The high profits generated in the above scenario by our sellers raising prices serves to attract new firms and resources to the sector. Supply is further increased by the actions of the managers seeking ways to increase output. As supply increases so the balance of power begins to move away from the supplier. Once demand and supply are more or less balanced, management has to change its priorities. Output is now taking care of itself. Success (and profits) will be ensured if a buyer can be found for the goods being produced.

Firms are still producing the goods and services they think the customer wants, but now they use promotional techniques like advertising and selling to 'push' the product at the customers – see Fig. 1.3.

This stage of business development is characterized by a *sales-oriented* management culture.

This phase of management thinking is frequently confused with a marketing or customer-oriented one. It is commonly assumed that marketing is simply a collective term for promotion. This sales-oriented approach to business is therefore easily mistaken as marketing. The result of this ignorance about the real nature of marketing is serious and creates a number of pitfalls.

- Marketing is relegated to a functional activity with little, and sometimes no senior management representation. Emphasis is placed on ad hoc, tactical promotional activities which tend to be neither an efficient nor an effective use of resources.
- Management kids itself that it 'has' marketing, so remains unaware of the danger of losing business and market share to competitors who actually do make the transition to customer orientation and so are better able to satisfy customer needs.
- Products are pushed at customers who do not really want them – a very expensive process, with promotional spending increasing costs. This reduces competitiveness and exposes the business to a greater loss of customers.

Fig 1.3

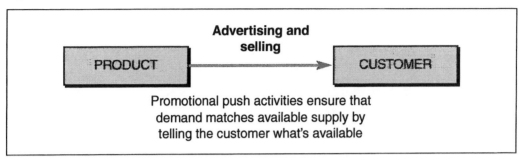

Advertising and selling

PRODUCT → CUSTOMER

Promotional push activities ensure that demand matches available supply by telling the customer what's available

Fig 1.4 From product to sales orientation

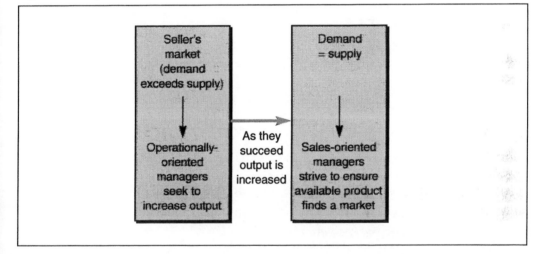

Seller's market (demand exceeds supply)

Demand = supply

Operationally-oriented managers seek to increase output

As they succeed output is increased

Sales-oriented managers strive to ensure available product finds a market

So, as the balance of demand and supply changes (see Fig. 1.4), so the critical success factors (CSF) change from increasing the production of output to shifting stock.

Customer orientation

Once again history shows that this new balance in the marketplace is unlikely to last long. External environmental changes, which cannot be controlled by managers, relentlessly increase supply. Driven, for example, by technological advances or political changes which open up markets to new competitors, supply across the mature industries of the world has continued to expand until marketplace after marketplace is faced with a *buyer's market*.

In a buyer's market supply exceeds demand. Some firms will fail to find buyers for the goods they have made or the services they offer. They will have used up scarce resources ineffectively and will go out of business gradually. Only when faced with this complete reversal in the balance of power does the manager *have* to rediscover the customer and recognize that satisfying customer needs is critical to the organization's success – see Fig. 1.5. For the business which has traditionally placed the product before the customer this is a dramatic change indeed.

Market research, not advertising and selling, is the real hall-mark of a customer-oriented approach to business. Customers' views are actively sought and the organization uses its exper-tise and skill to find profitable ways of satisfying those needs. The company must see its role as serving the customer.

You can still find examples of organizations at different stages of the continuum shown in Fig. 1.6. The dynamic which changes management's attitude comes only when the demand and supply balance changes.

Fig 1.5

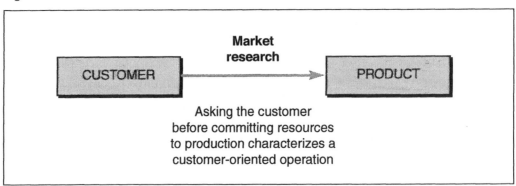

CUSTOMER

Market research

PRODUCT

Asking the customer
before committing resources
to production characterizes a
customer-oriented operation

Fig 1.6 Customer orientation

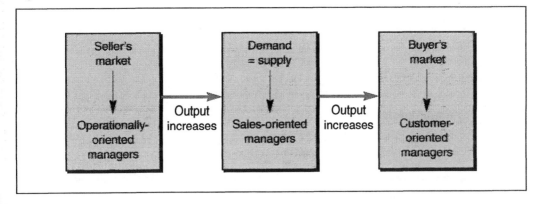

!!!
- Do not make the mistake of confusing the ends with the means.
- Marketing promotes customer satisfaction because in a competitive environment it is the only way of ensuring that the organization and its stakeholders achieve their objectives.
- A marketing approach is a means to an end – exchange must still be mutually beneficial, with both the customer and organization being satisfied.

---

eg
The driving force of deregulation
In the public sector of economic activity the main catalyst for change has been deregulation of markets. In Europe, telecommunications firms have been subjected to open-market competition, and market-style competition has been introduced to a variety of public sector providers. The results have the same impact – once customers have a choice, providers must pay attention to their needs, priorities and preferences.

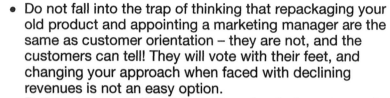

- Do not fall into the trap of thinking that repackaging your old product and appointing a marketing manager are the same as customer orientation – they are not, and the customers can tell! They will vote with their feet, and changing your approach when faced with declining revenues is not an easy option.
- Better managers will anticipate the advent of a consumer's market if they are not already operating in one and will manage the necessary culture change ahead of being forced to do so.

The recession of the late 1980s and early 1990s forced a number of companies to re-evaluate their true business orientation and management philosophies. The steady increase in supply caused by technology and removal of international trade barriers was reinforced by a severe recession, reducing demand and enlarging the gap between buyers and sellers. The buyer's market bit hard. Many organizations failed to survive.

The real thing?
In the mid-1990s the rebellion led by UK grocery retailers, complaining that brand wars between manufacturers offered little value added to them, resulted in giants like PepsiCo and Coca-Cola being faced with increased competition from retailer-sponsored brands like Sainsbury's Classic and Virgin Cola. Had these manufacturing companies recognized and responded earlier to the needs of their retailer customers, a rather different outcome may have resulted.

Societal orientation

The marketing philosophy preaches 'mutually beneficial exchange' – the needs of both provider and user being satisfied. This may not be the end to the challenges facing the manager of the future.

Concerns about the environment and the wider needs of society are gaining greater coverage. Today individuals cannot expect to have needs satisfied if this is at the expense of the well-being of others. These demands for broader considerations come from customers themselves and so represent a new set of demands which managers will need to satisfy.

Success in the future (Fig. 1.7) is likely to be achieved when managers find ways to combine the scarce resources in their control in ways which:

- satisfy the identified needs of individual customers (effective)
- do not damage community or global interests (socially endorsed)
- achieve the organization's objectives (efficient).

Fig 1.7 The third dimension

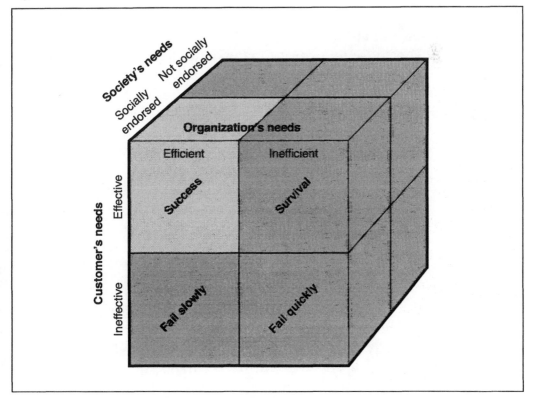

Management's task will be increasingly more demanding, and the skills of marketing planning will become even more critical.

What is the philosophy of management in your business?

Take a few minutes to think about your own organization or others with which you are familiar. Ask yourself:

- What is the focus of attention for managers?
- Is the business organized around the operational activities, sales or the customers?
- Do customers in your market have a choice?
- Do you spend resources on research and have mechanisms to generate two-way communication with customers?
- Are your customers/users satisfied?
- Is the organization achieving its objectives?
- How would you assess the current orientation, and does it need to change?

Checklist

The following questions will help you to establish your orientation.

1. Do you have a marketing champion represented in senior management?
2. Is marketing a 'department', or does it integrate closely with all other departments?
3. Do you regularly take your customers' views into account to improve your products and services?
4. Do you have difficulty achieving budgets that have not taken account of changes in the marketplace?
5. Is your mission statement meaningful, and relevant, or is it ignored by most people?
6. Do you make use of sales information to help you market more products?
7. Do your marketing people know anything about the needs of customers in your markets?

8. Do your marketing people spend more than 20 per cent of their time with customers?
9. Do you know what happens to your goods/services once they have gone out of your door?
10. Do you ever thank customers personally?
11. Do you ever ask your customers why they bought from you – or why they didn't?
12. Are you or your staff briefed on product sales or customer satisfaction?

The implications of change

You may by now have recognized the need for a change in the approach and attitude of your organization to the marketplace, or you may already be in the process of managing such a change, but as already indicated this is not an insignificant operation. Culture change is a slow process, requiring a fundamental shift in the attitude of both managers and customer contact staff. Achieving a customer-oriented organization requires commitment and investment. It requires change, not so much in what is done, but in the more intangible aspects of how it is done.

In traditional organizational structures managers are separated from customers and operational staff by multiple layers of middle and junior managers, and usually an equal number of floors, with senior staff carefully cocooned on the top floor. Communication is usually one-way, forced down functional chimneys, with accountants talking only to accountants, marketers to marketers, and so on – see Fig. 1.8.

Technology has provided the opportunity for radical change in the structure of organizations. Computer technology and improved communications have enabled many layers of management to be removed. This 'delayering' has flattened out the traditional pyramid and immediately brought senior

Fig 1.8 The traditional hierarchical organization structure

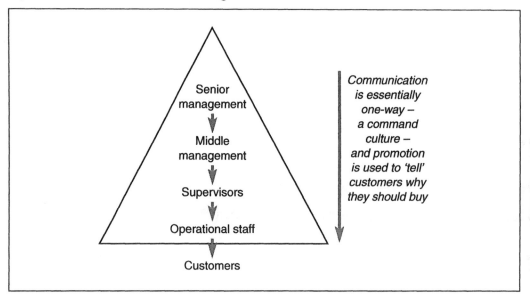

managers into closer proximity to the customers and those serving them – see Fig. 1.9. This is clearly a good thing.

Whilst technology has enabled this dramatic change, it was driven by the cost-cutting demands of the early 1990s recession. Managers were an expensive resource and once they were perceived to be no longer adding real value to the business process they were prime targets for redundancy.

Fig 1.9 The new model organization structure

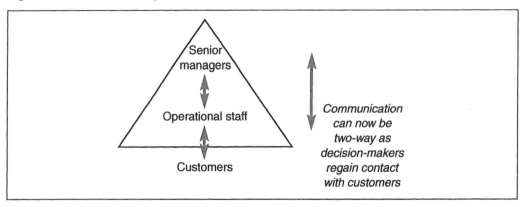

It was this same recession that reduced demand and increased over-supply in sector after sector. Senior managers who had now regained a sight of the customer in their flatter structure began to address the issue of how best to ensure customers' needs were established as the focus for organizational efforts. In other words, the now more efficient structures sought ways of making sure their efforts were equally effective.

This propensity was underscored as the diminishing opportunities for cost cutting in a 'lean' operation made it clear that revenue growth would be the key to profitability.

But the necessary culture change this required literally meant the organization had to be stood on its head – see Fig. 1.10. Driven by two complementary forces, the marketing push of customer orientation and the quest for quality, managers have found that improvements to achieve one will support the other.

Fig 1.10 Free flowing structure

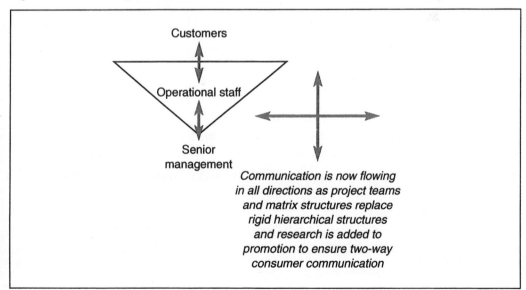

Customers

Operational staff

Senior
management

*Communication is now flowing
in all directions as project teams
and matrix structures replace
rigid hierarchical structures
and research is added to
promotion to ensure two-way
consumer communication*

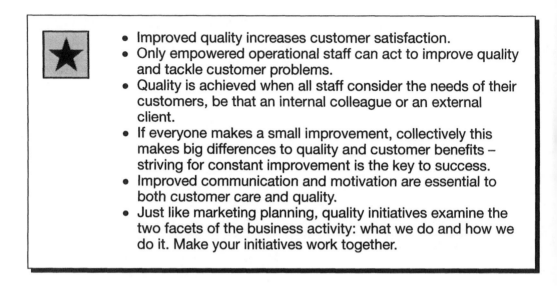

- Improved quality increases customer satisfaction.
- Only empowered operational staff can act to improve quality and tackle customer problems.
- Quality is achieved when all staff consider the needs of their customers, be that an internal colleague or an external client.
- If everyone makes a small improvement, collectively this makes big differences to quality and customer benefits – striving for constant improvement is the key to success.
- Improved communication and motivation are essential to both customer care and quality.
- Just like marketing planning, quality initiatives examine the two facets of the business activity: what we do and how we do it. Make your initiatives work together.

A storm of initiatives?

Do not let an array of business initiatives distract you. Many managers want to dismiss marketing as 'the flavour of the month'; last month it was appraisals and next it will be quality. At the same time, many fall into the trap of seeing the ongoing demand for improved performance – *more from less* – as being in direct conflict with these other fashions in management thinking.

In fact all of these initiatives are dimensions of the same basic philosophy – they represent part of a virtuous circle which planners are seeking to achieve – see Fig. 1.11. The only debate is where best to start – quality or marketing?

Fig 1.11 The virtuous circle of planning

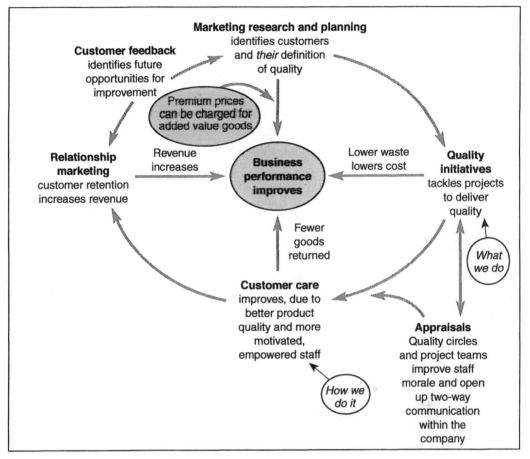

Introducing a customer-oriented culture

How is your organization structured? Are objectives set around products or customers? If staff are set objectives and allocated resources (and bonuses) based on the sales of X, Y and Z products, it is not surprising if they make decisions based on products, not customers. If you instead set objectives for increasing sales revenue from this segment of the market, staff will inevitably begin to focus on the needs of those customers and what additional opportunities exist for doing business with them.

Relationships not transactions

Once you have recognized that in mature markets customers are scarce, the importance of retaining them becomes clear. Building relationships means establishing long-term involvements – helping clients solve their problems. Tomorrow's income and today's loyalty have a higher value than a quick one-off sale of an inappropriate product today. Relationships not transactions are the key to success.

Work out the average value of a single transaction with a customer in your organization.

Now calculate what that customer is worth if he or she becomes loyal to you and buys exclusively from you over the rest of his or her life, or even the next three years.

Add an element to take account of the fact that this satisfied customer may introduce several others who also become loyal users.

Relationship marketing helps you to get more business from fewer customers – a good strategy when it's the customers who are scarce! Getting the organization to think about relationship building means planning for customers not products and allocating resources to customer segments.

In the system in Fig. 1.12, plans are made based on products A, B and C, and sales targets for each product would be set for the markets 1, 2 and 3. Achieving those targets may mean pushing inappropriate products at the customers. It also means that customers in market 1 may have three lots of promotional contact with the company and there is no one responsible for maximizing cross sell.

Fig 1.12 Planning focused on products

In this instance decisions are driven by considerations of *what* and *how much* we want to sell.

Market \ Product	A	B	C
1			
2			
3			
Objectives	X	Y	Z

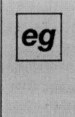

A change in style

This approach to planning was the classical style of the fast-moving consumer goods sector with its product and brand managers. Increasingly these are being replaced by key account and category managers charged with managing market segments and client groups, maximizing income, working in partnerships to build new product/service opportunities and offering a single point of contact.

Simply turning this product/market matrix around (see Fig. 1.13 overleaf) means that market or category managers working closely with clients can forecast what sales of which products can be achieved with their segment.

Products are now produced in response to customer demand, reducing the waste of developing products the customer does not value highly.

Pro-active not reactive

Because managers are closer to the customers, with an established relationship, they are much better positioned to forecast

Fig 1.13 Planning focused on customers

Here, production decisions and resource allocation are based on *what* and *how much* the customer wants to buy. Research focuses on possible future customer needs.

Product \ Market	1	2	3	Future opportunities	Objectives
A					X
B					Y
C					Z

future needs, developments and requirements. Better customer research and a partnership approach allows managers to anticipate change rather than being forced to react to events which had not been forecast.

Pro-active management is one of the advantages of a stronger marketing planning culture. Anticipation of the changing market environment (for you and your customers) and early demand forecasts give managers more opportunity to control changes which may be necessary. Firefighting can be exciting but it is also stressful and exhausting and inevitably leads to wasted resources. The intention of planning is to give you more control over an uncertain future – taking more of the risk out of business and improving the chances of successfully achieving your objectives.

For the busy manager, and the organization wanting to improve its performance, the key is to get *more from less*. The rationale for a strong marketing planning culture is clear – it provides the blueprint for success, offering the frameworks, tools and techniques for efficient and effective employment of those scarce organizational resources. In the following chapters we will examine how this can be achieved in your business.

Implementing a customer-oriented culture

- Start by clearly identifying the current and prevailing culture – if it is not focused on satisfying customer need, develop a plan for change.
- Do not be too ambitious or too impatient. Cultural change takes time – up to seven years is the typical estimate.
- Change has to start from the top. Senior managers have to be convinced and genuinely committed to the changes needed – they need to promote and endorse change.
- Do not simply rush out and employ a marketing professional. Simply grafting a marketing function on to a product-oriented culture will push you towards promotional, not customer orientation. If you want to take marketing seriously your marketer must be a board-level appointment.
- Use an external facilitator or consultant to help 'sell' the changes to an unwilling management. If you are doing the job yourself be well prepared with evidence of the inefficiency and ineffectiveness of the current approach, cases of marketing successes in your business and industry, and the benefits of change.
- Involve operational staff in the process. Discuss and promote the needs for and benefits of change for them. Dealing with satisfied customers is nearly always a better experience than fielding complaints.
- Consider using quality initiatives as a mechanism for implementing change within your business.
- Undertake detailed research with customers to identify their perceptions of you and their needs. Qualitative work and focus groups are most effective for this. Establish priorities for action.
- Organize staff around customer groups rather than products and get plans produced for each. If necessary produce a matrix structure, allocating client responsibility to individual staff who also have a functional role – i.e. ask them to wear two hats. Allocate resources accordingly.
- Open up communication channels to ensure that management listens to customers and staff and doesn't just tell them what to do or buy.
- Use appraisal systems to identify training and skills gaps, and empower operational staff to take more responsibility for quality and customer care. Reward them accordingly.
- Remember to measure the impact of your changes by establishing performance benchmarks today.

A planning review

If you want to undertake an audit of your current approach to planning you can use your responses to the following statements as a framework for that review. Modify these questions to meet the needs of your organization. You may want to ask questions of colleagues, senior managers and operational staff to compare your perceptions with theirs.

- We take planning seriously, allocating time and effort to the production of realistic, practical plans.

Score	1	2	3	4	5
	totally untrue	a little true	partly true	mostly true	very true

- Staff at all levels and across all functions contribute to the development of the business plan.

Score	1	2	3	4	5
	totally untrue	a little true	partly true	mostly true	very true

- All staff are aware of the broad business objectives, our vision and our strategy for achieving it.

Score	1	2	3	4	5
	totally untrue	a little true	partly true	mostly true	very true

- The business plan is put into action via a number of integrated marketing plans developed for each key *customer* segment.

Score	1	2	3	4	5
	totally untrue	a little true	partly true	mostly true	very true

- All plans are working documents referred to regularly and modified as necessary.

Score	1	2	3	4	5
	totally untrue	a little true	partly true	mostly true	very true

- We take positive steps to learn from our own planning activities. We take time to review and debrief past plans before moving forward to the next plan.

Score	1	2	3	4	5
	totally untrue	a little true	partly true	mostly true	very true

- There are well-established mechanisms and processes for taking into account customers' views, needs and preferences when planning and sharing that feedback across the organization.

Score	1	2	3	4	5
	totally untrue	a little true	partly true	mostly true	very true

- Budgets are allocated on the basis of what resources are needed to implement a specified plan, not on what we had last year or our share!

Score	1	2	3	4	5
	totally untrue	a little true	partly true	mostly true	very true

The maximum score is 40. Above 30 and you are well on your way to establishing a strong marketing planning culture. Below, and there is still some way to go. I hope hints and tips in the rest of this book will help.

CHAPTER 2

Unravelling the planning puzzle

Establishing a planning sequence

The problem with plans and planning

The hierarchy of plans

A planning sequence

Reviewing the planning sequence

How long does it take?

Planning as an activity

A planning challenge

Establishing a planning sequence

Amongst managers and management students alike the actual process of developing market-oriented business plans is a cause of some confusion. What do you do first? What is the planning sequence? Surely the business plan must come before a marketing or promotional plan? Most of this confusion is generated because often practitioners and frequently many management writers fail to distinguish clearly between the process of planning and the outputs of that process – the hierarchy of business and functional plans.

In this chapter we will:

- unravel the planning process and establish a step-by-step guide to planning
- develop the framework for a plan
- distinguish between business, marketing and tactical plans, and examine the purpose of this hierarchy
- clarify the terminology of planning and its meaning
- provide a framework for you to produce your own planning timetable.

The problem with plans and planning

The problem with planning is the time spent in preparation – hours of time which are invested in the process but do not show up in the finished product, i.e. the plan. It is like decorating a room. All the shopping, choosing and selecting of a colour scheme, the sanding down and stripping off that goes on behind the scenes and at the end it seems no one is aware of the effort that went into the finished room. But, of course, that is not the true picture. The quality of the preparation is reflected in the quality and success of the end product. The same is true of business planning.

As much as 80 per cent of your time and effort will go into the process of planning. Producing the final plan is just the tip of the iceberg, but the quality of your preparation will show in the effectiveness and success of the plans you implement.

- Many managers treat planning as an extra and perhaps unwelcome task that they are expected to complete annually. They allocate time for the writing of the plan but fail to recognize the effort needed to undertake the process thoroughly.
- As a result many plans are superficial, rushed and only pay lip service to what should be the central, not peripheral, activity of managers.
- The steps of preparation take time, and a calendar for planning needs to reflect this and allow for the preparation lead in.

The hierarchy of plans

There is a definite hierarchy of plans, which runs from the business plan to detailed tactical plans. It is commonly depicted in the format shown in Fig. 2.1 (overleaf), indicating that one plan is created after the other.

The size of your organization will determine how formalized and detailed each of these plans are, but even in a one-person business it should be possible to identify a plan for publicity and promotional activity, marketing plans and a clear business plan.

You can see from the hierarchy that the functional or operational level plans of marketing, finance, human resources and operations flow from the business plan. These functional plans themselves lead to tactical level plans like communications and public relations for the marketing team, and recruitment and training plans amongst the human resources group.

Fig 2.1 Hierarchy of plans

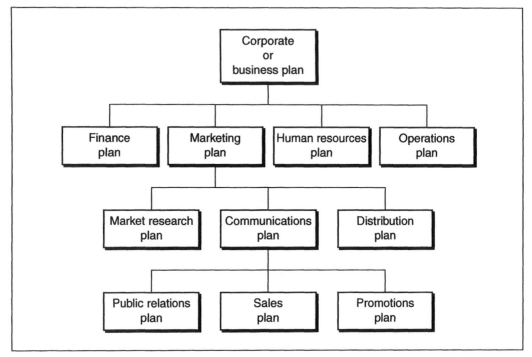

In one sense this hierarchy is true and it reflects the pecking order of the finished plans. It is certainly not possible to write an effective marketing plan unless the business plan has established clear objectives and strategic direction for the business. Similarly the public relations plan must be derived

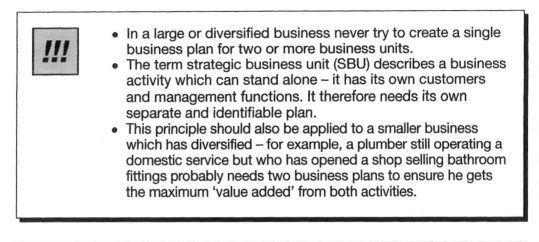

- In a large or diversified business never try to create a single business plan for two or more business units.
- The term strategic business unit (SBU) describes a business activity which can stand alone – it has its own customers and management functions. It therefore needs its own separate and identifiable plan.
- This principle should also be applied to a smaller business which has diversified – for example, a plumber still operating a domestic service but who has opened a shop selling bathroom fittings probably needs two business plans to ensure he gets the maximum 'value added' from both activities.

from a marketing plan which spells out the market segments being targeted and the overall objectives for each.

It is the specified objectives and strategies of the plan above that direct and co-ordinate the efforts of those in the plan below, thus ensuring synergy.

> **!!!**
> - The problem with this hierarchy is that many managers fall into the trap of trying to mimic it in their planning process.
> - Business plans are produced in splendid isolation and are fed down to the operational level managers who in turn magic up marketing and finance plans – too often with no reference to colleagues or subordinates.
> - In the worst cases managers are expected to produce their plans with only the vaguest notion of what is included in the business plan – as though this has no bearing on their activities.

Plans are intended to integrate the efforts of the organization and cannot be produced effectively in water-tight units. Information and decisions must flow freely back and forth, and up and down the business throughout the planning sequence.

Management cannot decide to expand into a new market without checking that there are the financial resources to do this and that the market potential makes it worthwhile. Plans must be developed in light of the overall strengths and weaknesses of the organization if they are to be realistic. They must also take account of the changing external environment if they are to have any chance of being achieved. An appropriate planning process will provide the mechanisms and sequence which enables planning to be both bottom up and top down.

Solid plans are based on a detailed understanding of the three Cs – capabilities, customers and competitors – as shown in Fig. 2.2.

Fig 2.2 The 3Cs

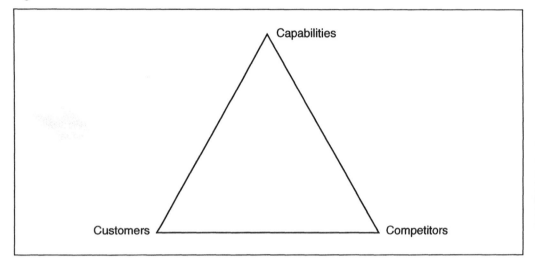

A planning sequence

Instead of looking at the relationship of the finished plans, let us consider the planning process, the actions and activities involved in producing the plans. We can examine the sequence of steps which must be taken to produce first a business plan and then a marketing plan – see Fig. 2.3.

Step 1 The functional audits

The production of a business plan should start with each functional area of the organization producing a detailed analysis of its own strengths and weaknesses. This audit stage must be detailed and wherever possible quantified (see chapter 4). For example, high staff turnover is a weakness, but it is important to know how much of a weakness and how significant that is. If our staff turnover was 15 per cent, compared with an industry benchmark of 8 per cent, we have a weakness which needs addressing.

The marketing department would be analyzing and evaluating the strengths and weaknesses of the marketing activity

Fig 2.3

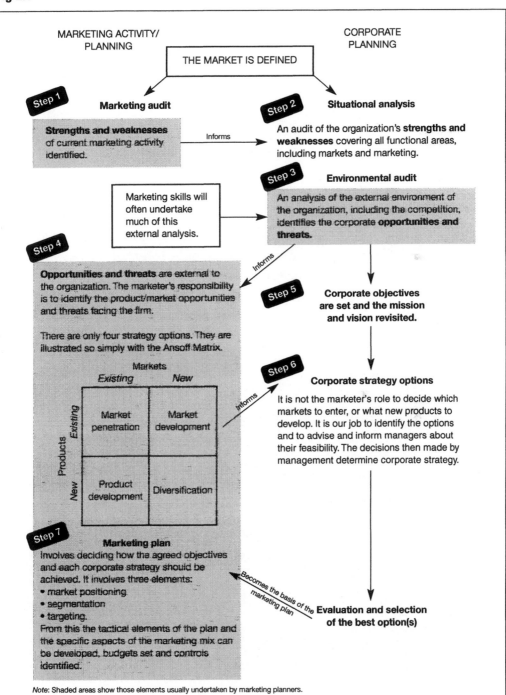

MARKETING ACTIVITY/
PLANNING

CORPORATE
PLANNING

THE MARKET IS DEFINED

Step 1   **Marketing audit**

Strengths and weaknesses
of current marketing activity
identified.

Informs

Step 2   **Situational analysis**

An audit of the organization's **strengths and
weaknesses** covering all functional areas,
including markets and marketing.

Marketing skills will
often undertake
much of this
external analysis.

Step 3   **Environmental audit**

An analysis of the external environment of
the organization, including the competition,
identifies the corporate **opportunities and
threats.**

Step 4

Opportunities and threats are external to
the organization. The marketer's responsibility
is to identify the product/market opportunities
and threats facing the firm.

There are only four strategy options. They are
illustrated so simply with the Ansoff Matrix.

Informs

Step 5   **Corporate objectives
are set and the mission
and vision revisited.**

Markets

	Existing	*New*
Existing	Market penetration	Market development
New	Product development	Diversification

Products

Step 6   **Corporate strategy options**

Informs

It is not the marketer's role to decide which
markets to enter, or what new products to
develop. It is our job to identify the options
and to advise and inform managers about
their feasibility. The decisions then made by
management determine corporate strategy.

Step 7   **Marketing plan**

Involves deciding how the agreed objectives
and each corporate strategy should be
achieved. It involves three elements:
• market positioning
• segmentation
• targeting.
From this the tactical elements of the plan and
the specific aspects of the marketing mix can
be developed, budgets set and controls
identified.

Becomes the basis of the marketing plan

**Evaluation and selection
of the best option(s)**

Note: Shaded areas show those elements usually undertaken by marketing planners.

during this step of the planning sequence. Details of customer awareness and perceptions, as well as our competitive position vis-à-vis pricing, availability, product quality, promotion and customer care, would be included.

Step 2 Compiling a situational analysis

This detailed analysis is used to inform the situational analysis of the business. This is quite literally a compilation of the functional audits which provides an evaluation of the business strengths and weaknesses, i.e. factors that are the controllable internal factors of the current position. Image, staff morale, poor productivity and so on are all internal issues that can be influenced by management action. Internal factors are therefore described as controllable. This is not to imply that these factors can be tackled easily or changed quickly, but they are within management's sphere of influence.

Strengths and weaknesses
Do not automatically assume that all weaknesses identified are equally serious and require the same management response. Some, like cashflow, will be more important than others. An analysis of strengths and weaknesses requires weighting and sorting further if it is to be of real value to management – see Fig. 2.4.

This process of sorting can help managers to identify priorities for action and contribute to breaking down the barriers between analysis and action.

Besides bringing together the evaluation of all the functional areas of the business this situational analysis must also include the corporate dimensions – for example, the qualities of the management team, the culture of the organization and the value of management information systems and planning processes.

Fig 2.4 Analysis of strengths and weaknesses

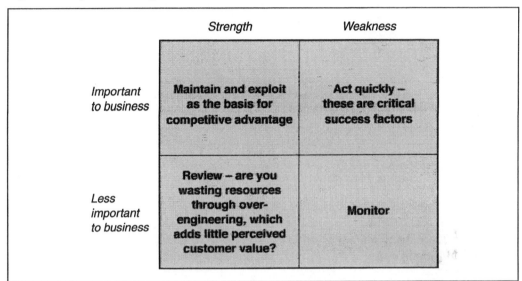

	Strength	*Weakness*
Important to business	**Maintain and exploit as the basis for competitive advantage**	**Act quickly – these are critical success factors**
Less important to business	**Review – are you wasting resources through over-engineering, which adds little perceived customer value?**	**Monitor**

Step 3 The environmental audit

The situational analysis is the first part of the corporate audit – the total business stock-take, which answers the question, 'where are we now?'

Once the internal analysis is complete, the business must consider the external influences upon it. This is done by completing an environmental audit. The factors reviewed in this part of the process are largely uncontrollable but can have significant effects on the business. It is changes in the environment which essentially change the fortunes of an organization. Those who fail to respond to such developments will fail to thrive and may not even survive. The more forward looking the management team, the more likely it is that it will have anticipated environmental changes and will have the opportunity to respond pro-

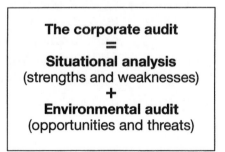

The corporate audit
=
Situational analysis
(strengths and weaknesses)
+
Environmental audit
(opportunities and threats)

actively to them, taking advantage of windows of opportunity and preparing the business to withstand threats.

A surprising number of organizations of all sizes quite openly admit that they plan their future without consideration of the environment. This seems an unnecessarily risky and ill-informed approach to business. It is equivalent to the ostrich sticking its head in the sand when threatened.

An economic surprise?
Many companies were apparently caught out by the economic recession of the late 1980s. The boom years preceeding it appeared to have caused managers to forget the existence of the business cycle. Booms are followed by recessions and depressions as surely as winter follows summer. The more recent bout of 'Asian Flu' has similarly been met by surprise despite few examples of economies maintaining sustained growth without feeling trade cycle impact.

In the late 1980s the downturn in economic fortunes was not hard to predict, but giant organizations like developer Olympia and York and retailers like UK company Queensway, and seemingly all the high street retail banks, appear to have been taken by this economic surprise.

Diverse influences

Environmental factors include a wide variety of influences on the business, including many factors which often change less predictably than the economy and sometimes very dramatically, like political change and technological developments, legislative reviews, strategic alliances and global warming. Managers must be alert to a diversity of influences on their fortunes. We will examine some of the approaches and sources for doing this in chapter 5.

Step 4 Analyzing the information

Once the environmental audit is complete, the information in it requires processing so it is of relevance and value to the business planners. It is usually the task of marketers to translate these external opportunities and threats into specific opportunities for product sales or market growth and to identify any threats to the core business.

- Do not forget that the competition is also an uncontrollable influence whose decisions and strategies are likely to affect your fortunes directly.
- A business must get to know the competition as well as itself and play to its strengths, where possible, highlighting and exploiting competitors' weaknesses.
- Competitors are not always in the same industry as you. The loyal customer may not be choosing between a meal at your restaurant and one at a competitor down the road, but between a night at the theatre and a meal out. Do not make the mistake of failing to recognize who the real competitors are. This is only certain if you define the business you are in carefully in terms of customer needs, *not* products.

The environmental audit can be reviewed by applying the question, 'so what?'

- So what if there is a change in government?
- So what if 90 per cent of households have access to the Internet by 2003?
- So what if there is an increase in competition from the Far East, or a merger between two key industry players?

What does it mean for our business?

The outcomes of this review can conveniently be logged using the Ansoff Matrix (see Fig. 2.5), a marketing model

Fig 2.5 Ansoff Matrix

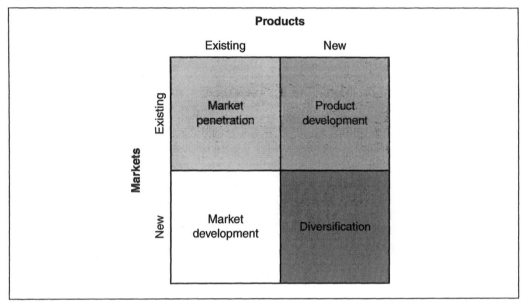

which captures in one grid the only strategic growth alternatives open to any organization:

- existing products to existing customers (market penetration)
- existing products to new markets (market development)
- new products to existing customers (product development)
- new products to new markets (diversification).

The challenge during this fourth step of the planning process is to capture all the possible opportunities and to explore thoroughly all the threats. There is no need to be critical – evaluation and selection come at the next stage. Creative ideas and new approaches can emerge from an unblinkered review of the changing marketplace and these may provide the opportunity to win competitive advantage.

The marketing team has now completed the audit of its activities concurrently with the corporate audit. Strengths and weakness were identified at Step 1 and the opportunities and threats, expressed in terms of products and markets, completed at Step 4.

- Note the crucial link between the external environment and the current and potential products made and markets served. Changes in the environment, like new technology, make products obsolete. Political changes threaten market share by introducing new competitors, and economic growth creates the chance to introduce a luxury version of your standard model.
- It is changes in the environment which are the dynamic forces changing the nature of business activity. Take time to review your marketplace. What has changed in the environment over the last 10 years and how have the products and markets changed as a result?

Take care to keep external environmental changes, which must be responded to, clear from product market opportunities which can be exploited.

Step 5 Establishing the corporate objectives

Working with the input of functional managers, the business team must now decide on realistic objectives for the next three to five years. To be of any value these must be quantified, and for a private sector organization this would usually be expressed in terms of profit, or return on capital employed. For the not-for-profit sectors, corporate objectives would be expressed in terms of other quantifiable benefits to the organization's stakeholders – for example, operations concluded, funds raised or crimes detected. This objective *must* be set in light of the environmental audit to ensure it is realistic.

Once the objective is set, the difference between this objective and a forecast of what would happen to business if it changed nothing, i.e. stuck with its current products, markets and marketing spend, can be calculated – as shown in Fig. 2.6.

Fig 2.6 The planning gap

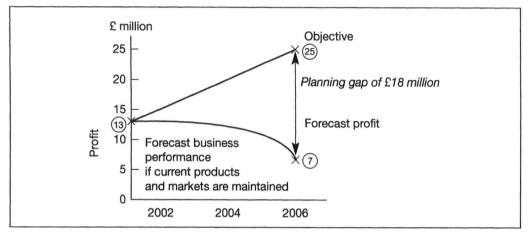

The current profits of £13 million in this example are forecast to show a decline of £6 million over the four years of the plan as a result of environmental changes. The company has set an objective of £25 million profit by 2006. The difference between these two points – £18 million – is the size of the planning gap, i.e. the amount of new and replacement business which is needed to achieve the objective. It is the translation of identified threats which inform the bottom line of the planning gap.

 Quantification like this is fundamental to successful planning. It immediately gives managers a sense of the scale of the challenge and provides benchmarks for control as well as a basis for budget setting and resource allocation. Objectives must however be SMART – specific, measurable, achievable relevant and timed.

Step 6 Filling the planning gap

Managers must now decide which strategic options (identified in Step 4) are most suitable for filling this planning gap. Marketers might have been responsible for identifying the opportunity to expand business in South America, but the decision to do so is a corporate one not a marketing one.

!!!

- Do not let strategies be selected on the basis of strategy champions.
- Senior managers who sit around a table debating the merits of one alternative over another will be mainly subjective in their evaluation. This will not necessarily generate decisions in the best interests of the organization.

Strategy evaluation must be undertaken as objectively as possible. Techniques and models exist to help with this (see chapter 6) and marketing teams will contribute to the process with assessments of the feasibility of the various alternatives, based on analysis and research *not* gut feel.

Where are we now?

Completion of this step finalizes the development of the business strategy – the core of the business plan. This involves a detailed assessment of the current position and the environment, leading to the establishment of quantified objectives and the selection of a strategy or strategies which play to the identified strengths and are forecast to fill the planning gap. It is now up to the functional areas, including marketing, to implement this strategy.

Step 7 The marketing plan

Only when a corporate objective and strategy have been agreed is it possible to produce operational plans including the marketing plan. Once informed of the selected strategies, the marketing team can set about the task of implementation of the business plan by converting strategies into marketing plans (see chapters 7 and 8).

The marketing audit is already completed so the first task for the marketer is to take the corporate objective and translate it into terms the marketing team can relate to.

- Do not try to produce a single marketing plan for a single business plan. If you have more than one strategy you will need more than one plan.
- The more specific the focus of a marketing plan the more effective it will be.

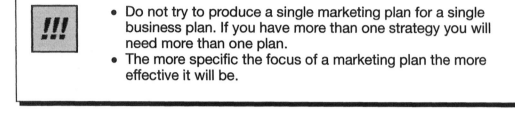

The job of each manager is to take the objectives set in the plan above them and turn it into terms that mean something to the teams expected to implement that part of the plan. Increasing return on capital employed by 3 per cent has no meaning to the salesforce, but asking them to increase sales by 400 cases a month does. They instantly have a sense of the scale of the challenge and know what is expected of them.

Marketing objectives

Marketing objectives might be expressed as revenue, sales, customer numbers, occupancy or market share, but always in some form which is relevant to the team.

Be careful of market share estimates, which can be a difficult objective to work with:

- Market share estimates may be unreliable and/or difficult to get.
- They depend on definitions of the market, which may change.
- The market may be growing or declining, so your share may not be a good reflection of performance – for example, you could have lower sales, but a bigger market share if the market was contracting. Remember the reason for planning is to match demand and available supply; fudging the numbers achieves little.

Marketing strategy
Marketers must mirror the steps of the corporate plan, identifying which segments of the market might be targeted to achieve the marketing objective, selecting the most appropriate and determining how best to position their offering to satisfy the needs of this group. Once segmentation and positioning are agreed then the marketing strategy is in place.

Marketing tactics
Details for implementation of this strategy are required, with plans for all elements of the marketing mix to ensure each reinforces the agreed positioning. The positioning map acts as the blueprint which ensures integration of the mix elements.

Controls
A **budget** based on the resources required to implement the above strategy and tactics must be set. This will then require an internal marketing plan to win the support of senior managers and the buy-in of those who will take responsibility for implementation.

> **!!!**
> - Budgets cannot be decided in isolation from the plans and neither should plans be shopping lists of how to spend this year's allocated budget.
> - Customer-oriented planning requires that resources are allocated on an 'objective and task' basis. In other words, this is what we want to achieve, this is what we must do to achieve it and these are the resources required to complete those tasks.

A **timetable** will promote action from the plan, again providing a useful bridge between the planning process and implementation. Written down and reviewed regularly, an action plan:

- reduces the wastage of resources because of poor sequencing of actions
- provides a measure against which progress can be readily assessed.

Fig 2.7 Recruiting new sales staff

	Action	Jan	Feb	Mar	Apr	May	Jun	Jul	Aug
Develop job description and personnel spec.	1	▨							
Place adverts	2		▨						
Sort replies and shortlist for interviews	3		▨						
Hold preliminary interviews	4			▨					
Final interviews and selection	5				▨				
Induction training	6						▨		
First assessment	7							▨	

Feedback is the third element of the control process. Managers must plan controls and feedback from the beginning. Measures against which performance of both the planning and the planning process can be assessed are critical to:

- provide advance warning of plans not working
- help managers learn from their own planning activities
- increase understanding of buyer behaviour in the market.

- Do not make the mistake of assuming that because a plan is written down it will inevitably work. Managers can easily make the mistake of producing plans written in tablets of stone.
- Plans are most unlikely to work out without adaptation and modification, because they have been developed with incomplete information based on forecasts of the future that will almost certainly prove to be wrong. You made decisions based on assumptions and forecasts. These need monitoring.
- The further ahead you are planning the more likely it is that your plans will require modification – but good managers are alert, flexible and prepared for contingencies.

Reviewing the planning sequence

As you can see, business plans cannot be developed in isolation but need close links with the functional areas of the business, not just marketing, but operations, finance and human resources as well. The planning steps are logical and easy to follow, but they take time as there is the need for communication up and down the organization at each stage – see Fig. 2.8. Planning effectively is an iterative process.

How long does it take?

For those of you anxious to produce a planning timetable you need rather more than just a sequence against which to plan your activities – you also need some indication of how long each step is likely to take. That will vary according to a number of factors:

- the size and complexity of your business
- the experience of planning and management information already in existence
- the resources you have available to help with the planning activity.

Fig 2.8 The planning timetable

As you have seen from Fig. 2.3 the process of planning is far from the neat sequential activity implied by the planning hierarchy.

Step 1 All operational areas, including marketing, audit their activities to identify strengths and weaknesses: the internal controllable factors. These are then communicated to the senior management team.

Step 2 Situational analysis combines all the information generated in Step 1 plus any uniquely corporate issues like culture and the evaluation of management strengths to produce a summary of the organization's strengths and weaknesses. These would be weighted and put into a priority order to identify critical success factors and limiting organizational factors.

Step 3 Having taken a detailed look at itself, the organization must now put itself into an environmental context. This identifies emerging opportunities and threats to the business.

Step 4 Marketers take this environmental audit and interpret its meaning in terms of products and markets. Changes in the environment may threaten traditional markets or open up new opportunities. Marketing's role is to identify all of these options – the opportunities represent the alternative strategies open to the business.

Step 5 Management reviews the business mission and vision, and sets quantified objectives which are realistic in light of the current position and forecast environment.

Step 6 Once informed of the options available, management must select between them. A process for evaluation on an objective basis is needed to ensure the most attractive option suited to the organization's strengths is selected as the corporate strategy. In reality most organizations or business units will adopt more than one strategy.

Step 7 Once selected, the agreed strategy is communicated to all operational level departments. Each is then responsible for creating a plan which will implement the agreed strategy. This is the starting point for the development of the marketing plan. For a multiple strategy approach multiple marketing plans are needed.

Time to plan
In the UK in the early 1990s the Department of Trade and Industry supported a number of initiatives to improve planning in small/medium-sized companies. It allocated 15 consultancy days for each of these projects. In these cases the management of each company would also be actively involved in working through the planning process, and so a further 5–10 days of time could usually be assumed. Altogether this amounted to something in the order of 25 days – a not insignificant proportion of any manager's diary, but perhaps an indication of why plans cannot just be squeezed in as an afterthought. Neither should they be attempted in too concentrated a space of time. Planning should be spread over months not weeks.

As a rule of thumb planning time should be allocated in the following proportions:

- internal situational analysis – 20 per cent
- external environmental audit – 20 per cent
- strategy identification, evaluation and selection – 30 per cent
- production and communication of plan – 30 per cent.

Use the checklist overleaf to help you to set a realistic timetable for your next business and marketing plans. Start backwards from when your plan is due to be submitted and set yourself a schedule for each stage. Remember that you will need to allow

- If your planning activities are relatively undeveloped, do not try to get the plans perfect first time – it isn't a reasonable goal.
- Do not allow the process to be held up because of a lack of competitor data, or inadequate management information. Instead, work through the process and make reasonable assumptions where necessary.
- You can always revise your plans in light of better information later, and your planning skills will improve over time.

time each week for other responsibilities, and space for seasonal peaks in activity, holidays, etc. should be built in. Most organizations should be working on at least a three-month lead time for producing their plan. In complex organizations with multiple strategies six months might be more realistic.

Due date

Step 7 Production and presentation of the marketing plan

- co-ordination of tactical marketing plans for each differentiated segment   _____
- confirmation of agreed marketing objectives and strategy for each selected business opportunity   _____

Step 6 Finalization of corporate strategy

- evaluation of feasibility of identified options   _____
- completion of necessary market research   _____
- evaluation of alternatives by management   _____

Step 5 Confirmation of corporate objectives and planning gap

- review and agreement of mission and vision   _____
- forecasts of likely demand   _____
- feedback from operational managers on the objectives set _____

Step 4 Identification of the alternative strategies open to the business   _____

Step 3 Environmental audit – including competitor and customer analysis   _____

Step 2 Situational audit   _____

Step 1 Functional area audits   _____

Over the following chapters we will work through the steps of producing a marketing strategy and plan in more detail. But before moving on there are a few terms and techniques which we have mentioned which should be more fully explained.

Planning as an activity

As indicated in chapter 1, planning is an everyday activity, which is not limited to the world of business or to one level of management within business. That can cause problems when you are faced with the terminology of planning – terminology which is as widely used in games and wars as in business. Terms like mission, strategy and tactics can cause confusion amongst managers because they are used at all levels. They refer not to an activity specific to a particular step of planning within the organizational hierarchy, but to a point in the planning process itself.

Objectives

These are always *what* is to be achieved. There has to be a goal or objective, which is of no use unless it is specific and quantified over time. A statement that we want to 'sell more' is completely inadequate. An objective that we want to sell 25 per cent of our current capacity level to the European market by 2006 is **quantified** over **time** and is **specific**. To be of help to planners this objective has to be **relevant** to those who will implement the plan and also perceived by them to be **achievable**. A financially based corporate objective of raising the return on capital employed needs translating to a marketing goal, based on market share, utilization levels or customer numbers, if it is to inform the marketing plan. Similarly, a market share objective needs turning into a sales volume target if it is to be meaningful to the sales team.

Strategy

This answers the question of how any agreed objective is to be achieved. The strategy of the plan is usually fairly brief, a broad statement of how we intend to deliver the objectives.

- At corporate level the strategy indicates the product and market opportunities selected – for example, to grow the business by 10 per cent through the addition of new digital technology services.
- Marketing strategy specifies how marketing objectives will be achieved. It requires decisions on the position to be adopted within the market and details of the segments to be targeted – for example, our new services will be premium priced and better quality, developed for the HQ corporate market.

Tactics

These provide the detail of the plan. At marketing level the plan involves details of each element of the marketing mix. In turn, the promotional plan includes details of all the elements of the communications mix. The tactics of the business plan are the various functional plans, including marketing.

Controls

These help us to check if we are on track. Control is a critical element of the process and one which should feature strongly in all plans. You should provide an indication of costs presented as a budget, a timetable of activity and the information you would need in order to monitor progress against your plan.

The above terms can be used in any plan, be it the business plan or sales plan. To clarify the hierarchical level of the plan you would need to confirm whose strategy or objectives you were referring to. This can be identified if you stop and think about who this is relevant to – see Fig. 2.9.

Fig 2.9 Who is the plan for?

	Corporate or business	Marketing	Promotion
Objectives are expressed in terms of:	profit or stakeholder benefits	customers, revenue or market share	awareness, attitude or action
Strategy confirms:	which products and which markets are to be targeted	which segments of customers and what positioning is to be adopted	whether a sales push or advertising pull approach is to be used
Tactics provide details summarized from:	the functional plans, including the marketing plan	plans for each element of the marketing mix	the individual plans for each element of communication activity
Controls exposed in terms of:	cost and revenue	market growth, average spend and cross sell	conversion and enquiry ratios

A planning challenge

Check your understanding of the planning terminology by matching the statements below with the descriptions that follow. All terms are used only once.

1 The manager of a chain of stores asks each manager to report only if sales are more than 5 per cent off budget.

2 The manager of a domestic cleaning firm decides to target detached properties in three suburban areas within her region.

3 The delicatessen retailer decided to move into party catering.

4 The board agree to try to achieve 27 per cent gross profit next year.

5 The sales team plans to achieve a conversion rate of 3:5 next quarter.

6 Promotional activities are developed to attract new users to the wine bar.

7 By establishing a prestige image and limited availability it is expected the product will appeal to a discerning group of customers.

8 Doubling market share was thought ambitious but not unrealistic in this growing market.

a corporate strategy (diversification)

b corporate objective

c sales objective

d promotional strategy (promotional pull)

e marketing objective

f marketing strategy (positioning)

g a control

h marketing strategy (segmentation)

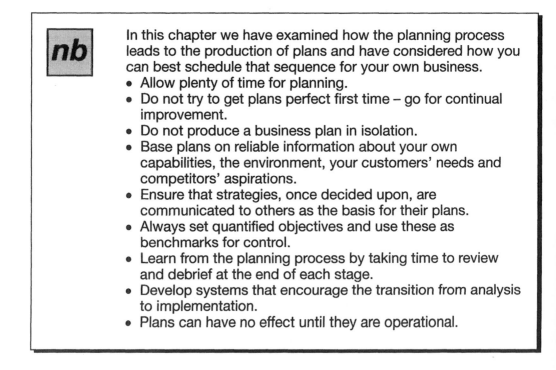

nb

In this chapter we have examined how the planning process leads to the production of plans and have considered how you can best schedule that sequence for your own business.

- Allow plenty of time for planning.
- Do not try to get plans perfect first time – go for continual improvement.
- Do not produce a business plan in isolation.
- Base plans on reliable information about your own capabilities, the environment, your customers' needs and competitors' aspirations.
- Ensure that strategies, once decided upon, are communicated to others as the basis for their plans.
- Always set quantified objectives and use these as benchmarks for control.
- Learn from the planning process by taking time to review and debrief at the end of each stage.
- Develop systems that encourage the transition from analysis to implementation.
- Plans can have no effect until they are operational.

Answers – A planning challenge

1 = g   2 = h   3 = a   4 = b   5 = c   6 = d   7 = f   8 = e

CHAPTER 3

Informing the planners

Managing the information input

The value of information

Data or information

The marketing information system

Managing marketing research

Managing the information input

We are at the beginning of an information revolution, the extent of which few of us can really imagine. The rapid development of computer technology, its merging with telecommunications, and developments of virtual reality will have an enormous impact on the quantity and quality of information available to every manager. It will influence how, when and where decisions are made.

In businesses large and small, managers must now address the issue of information – what they have got, what they need and how they can use this resource better in order to gain and retain advantages over their competitors. Whilst there may still be information gaps limiting your planning and decision-making, information overload will be just as real a threat in the future.

In this chapter we will consider how to manage information – the raw material of planning. We will:

- examine the nature and characteristics of effective management information systems
- develop a system for pro-active information management
- consider how to audit existing information flows
- evaluate how managers can use information available to them.

The value of information

Information is an aid to decision-making, not a crutch for managers to rely on. Information does not guarantee that the decisions made will be right, but if it is reliable it can help reduce the chances of getting any decision wrong.

The problem is that managers are still generally unused to the volume and quality of information they can access. We have traditionally tended to be passive receivers of information and are not yet very sure about becoming more assertive prescribers of the information we want. This is quite a serious weakness because the passive information receiver runs two risks:

- being inundated with information of little or no value, which takes precious time and energy to sort and reject
- not having access to relevant and potentially available information which would improve the quality of his or her decision-making and be a real contribution to the planning process.

Audit your information flow over the next few days or weeks. Make a point of monitoring the information which you receive. If it is in paper form put it into three piles – useful, interesting and of no value. You can do the same by opening files for your electronic mail:

- What proportion of the information you receive do you use?
- Is there any identifiable pattern to this – for example, which senders send the most/least useful materials?
- How helpful is the format of the information you receive?
- How long did you spend considering and discarding irrelevant information?

Just 30 minutes a day is $2\frac{1}{2}$ hours a week – 100 hours in a 40-week year. Save that or a fraction of it and think what more productive uses you could put that time to. Work out your annual time wasted by being a passive information receiver. Now multiply that by the colleagues in your team.

Draw up a list of:

- information you regularly receive and need to see
- information you need to be able to access but do not need to see
- information you receive now but do not need to see.

Think also about the information you send and the recipients as 'customers'. Does it meet their needs, do they need it at all or in its current format? Set the 'information improvement initiative' in motion by taking steps to customize your own information output. Ask for feedback.

Perhaps not surprisingly, passive managers are unwilling to call for more information as they are struggling to cope with what is already on their desk. Positive action, therefore, has to be taken.

---

eg

Make the most of e-mail
Electronic mail – e-mail – is no longer a new facility for most managers and has spread rapidly. Managers may receive over 300 e-mails a day, the majority of which are not directly relevant. In the past they would not have been added to a circulation list, but with e-mail it is as easy to include everyone. It may only take a minute to open and discard a message but those minutes add up. Improved communication is vital for a successful business, but some discretion about the value of the messages sent is likely to be much appreciated.

Secondary sources of information are at your fingertips as you surf the Net and again data overload may be the biggest challenge faced.

Data or information

Managers need information, not data. To aid decision-making, data must be collected, analyzed and presented in a form and at a time that it can be of most use to the decision-maker. Last quarter's sales figures are of little help to the store manager five days after he had to submit next month's stock order.

The management information system (MIS) represents the activities, procedures, people and processes which contribute to the gathering, recording, processing, analyzing and for-matting of data within the business. One part of the MIS is the financial system of the business. Imagine the manager of a large retailer asking her accountant for information on the company's trading position for the week. Instead of a sum-mary of sales, broken down by department and an indication of costs and operating profit (management information), she receives a pile of till receipts and invoices received (data). You can see from the example how piles of data are of little help to the busy manager. The same would be true if the customer survey results turned up not as summary sheets but as the completed questionnaires!

Managers neither have the time nor necessarily the skills needed to analyze and process raw data. Increasingly this can be done in real time by computerized information systems. Electronic Point of Sale (EPS) provides the shopkeeper with analysis of sales by time of day, product category and customer value, whilst automatically updating stock inventories. Customer satisfaction surveys are recorded on-line from your seat on an aeroplane or via the TV screen in your hotel room.

The marketing information system

Whilst the MIS contains information on all aspects of the business performance and will be critical to completing the corporate level situational analysis, the Marketing Information System (MKIS) is a single part of MIS and generates information on the markets and marketing activity. It is this element of the MIS which is central to the marketing planning activity.

Developing an effective MKIS

Step 1 Assess information needs
An audit of the needs of marketing planners is the first step in developing or reviewing the MKIS.

Marketing managers need information to help them:

- *analyze* markets and opportunities
- *plan* marketing activities
- *implement* and *monitor* plans
- *control* the use of marketing resources.

Each manager needs to identify the decisions which must be taken regularly and any projects planned for the near future. They must consider:

- what information would help them make those decisions
- the degree of risk involved, i.e. what are the costs associated with making the wrong decision
- the frequency and experience of making this or similar decisions previously.

Cost versus risk

The greater the risk and/or the more unused to the decision you are the more information is needed to make the decision.

Degree of risk is not the only indicator. Every day you make the decision to cross the road. This is potentially very risky, but you have a system for collecting relevant information – looking and listening – and you make the decision quickly and routinely. The riskier the conditions the more data you process – for example, bad weather and dual-carriageway roads require more information than quiet backstreets.

In business a routine decision about packaging design would require much more information if you intended to offer the product on the Asian market for the first time.

Step 2 Source the information

Once needs have been identified, managers can look for ways of generating the information. Data will have to be collected to inform marketing planners about:

- the organization's performance and capabilities
- customers and their behaviour
- market intermediaries and their needs
- the prevailing external environment
- the competition
- other stakeholder groups interested in the business.

Some information may be required on a regular basis. This is usually referred to as continuous information, and it establishes trends and enables managers to forecast future patterns. Examples would be sales figures, perhaps correlated to weather information so the manager can forecast future sales of ice creams, or the sales of heating systems related to recorded temperatures. Such information enables promotional tactics to be tied into actual weather conditions – for example, commercials only broadcast when temperatures exceed or fall below a given temperature. Long-range weather forecasts would help managers plan stocking levels, and sales figures could be more accurately benchmarked against weather patterns because a key variable had been accounted for.

At other times marketers may need ad hoc information, i.e. information for a one-off decision, perhaps to help decide the colour of a revamped package design. In this case market research is most likely to be undertaken to provide this specific information.

Data and marketing information can be gained from four basic sources:

- *internal records* – including customer feedback, sales reports, inventory levels and so on. Information already being collected within the business for another purpose.
- *market intelligence* – usually based on external secondary sources of information forming the core of the continuous information flow used primarily to alert managers to changes in the external environment. Regular 'mystery shopping' trips would identify changes in competitor's pricing strategies, and demographic monitoring would identify shifts in population or segment size. Reports from the weather centre would flag global warming and political advisers would warn of potential legislation being proposed.

- *marketing research* – specific information gathering projects designed to provide managers with information to help them to make specific decisions – for example, whether to launch a new product or enter a new market.
- *statistical and computerized modelling* – the increase in available information and greater objectivity and training amongst managers means a growth in more 'scientific methods' being developed to support management decision-making. Calling on much of the same data as generated by the above sources, pricing models, correlation analysis, site selection models, game theory and similar methods are being actively used to improve marketing decision-making.

Opportunities opened up by virtual reality, enabling managers to trial new products and store layouts without first producing them are likely to increase dramatically the opportunities for analyzing and evaluating customer behaviour.

Step 3 Disseminating information

Once data is collected and processed, the information must be distributed to the decision-makers. Its availability at the right time and its delivery in a user-friendly format will now be critical to its usefulness and value.

Step 4 Information aids decision-making

At this final stage it is possible to begin evaluating whether the investment in information was or was not worthwhile. You can ask:

- Was the information used?
- Did it influence the decision made?
- Was the decision 'better' as a result of the information?
- How would the manager like to see this information improved?

- As with all aspects of business, providing information takes resources. Managers must always be alert to whether they can get more for less.
- Question the value of information you receive and make proposals to make it more useful and cost less.
- Be obsessed with the cost versus the benefit of all information you handle.

- Audit managers to identify their information needs.
- Find cost-effective sources of information.
- Provide and distribute information in a user-friendly format – ask for feedback from those you provide information to.
- Review and modify the information provided.
- Monitor the impact of better information on business performance.

Managing marketing research

As we have just identified, marketing research is just one source of information available to the business planner, but it is an important one which needs special attention. Marketing research often involves collecting primary data. That means undertaking research unique to your business to collect new data. It is a *very* expensive process and is usually conducted by a third party – a consultant or researcher.

- Do not assume marketing professionals are expert researchers – it is a specialist field. In the same way you would not expect your doctor necessarily to be a skilled surgeon.
- Smaller organizations often fall into the trap of thinking everyone can write a questionnaire – well, they can't. It is easy to end up with biased research full of errors and mistakes which will generate results more likely to hamper, not aid, your decision-making.

Need to know information

Before any research is undertaken, the manager must once more go through the process of identifying the information needs and considering ways in which this information can be obtained.

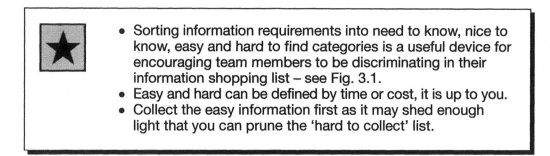

- Sorting information requirements into need to know, nice to know, easy and hard to find categories is a useful device for encouraging team members to be discriminating in their information shopping list – see Fig. 3.1.
- Easy and hard can be defined by time or cost, it is up to you.
- Collect the easy information first as it may shed enough light that you can prune the 'hard to collect' list.

Fig 3.1 Prioritize your information needs

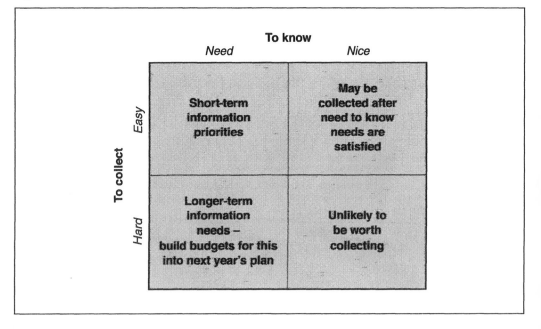

Managers can sometimes get almost obsessive about finding information which really is of only marginal help to decision-making. For example, a manager may ask, 'what share of the market do we have?' Unless it is over 80 per cent and there is little chance of further penetration does it really matter? Whether it is 3 per cent or 4 per cent, it will not significantly influence your strategy. There are plenty of customers to target, and finding out how many may be an expensive exercise – generating nice to know, but *not* need to know information.

The basics of marketing research

Assuming that you are using a market research specialist, you will not need much specialist knowledge to manage the research project, but some understanding of the basics may help you to make more informed decisions.

- *Secondary* sources of data should always be explored before undertaking primary research.
- *Primary* data can be collected by:
  - *observation*, which is particularly useful in retail environments
  - *experimentation*, for example, test marketing a new product
  - *survey*, which is not just people with clipboards, but also telephone- or postal-based questioning.
- The larger the research sample the more accurate your results are likely to be, and the more likely it is that the views of those sampled will reflect the opinions of the whole segment you are interested in. If you interview them all, it is a census, if only some, it is a *sample survey*. However, once you have a significant sample, more respondents will tend to escalate costs, *not* improve accuracy.
- Samples can be selected by a number of techniques but they fall broadly into two categories: probability (*random*)

samples and non-probability (*quota*) samples. Both can generate equally useful results if done properly, but quota is used more in business because it is more cost effective. A sample is drawn which reflects the characteristics of your segment. If, for example, you were interested in European youngsters aged 14–18 years, you may draw up your sample to reflect the proportion of people in this age group residing in each of the European countries.

- Standard formatted questions typical of questionnaire-based research is known as *quantitative* research. It is very useful for finding out factual information as it answers questions like: what? where? when? how? and how much?
- *Qualitative* methods are based on psychology and seek answers to the question, why? Sometimes referred to as unstructured or motivational research, it involves smaller groups drawn as a quota sample, using in-depth work that draws out behaviours and perceptions. A barrage of techniques exist, but the most common are in-depth interviews and group discussions. Sometimes qualitative work is done to help construct a quantitative research survey.

Selecting an agency

Market research agencies, like promotional ones, would normally expect to have a long-term relationship with a client. The selection process, therefore, is important. The management team need to draw up a list of criteria which are important to them. These will differ from organization to organization but might include:

- no competitive clients
- experience of our market or type of business
- range of skills and services offered
- importance of our work to them
- references from other clients
- location and geographic coverage
- availability.

Do not forget to check that you like the team. A clash of corporate cultures or personalities does not add value to this sort
of partnership.

Selection

Ask suppliers, other contacts and colleagues to recommend
possible agencies. Keep your eyes open in the trade press for
reports of successful firms, and use the *Yellow Pages* or trade
directories. Ask 10 to submit information about themselves,
shortlist them to three and ask to meet them.

- Ensure that you make the initial contact with the firms
  personally. Make notes of how you were handled and the
  speed of response; in other words conduct some mystery
  shopping research on the researchers.
- Visit them at their premises to get a feel for the business, its
  size, professionalism and the volume of work being done.

The brief

Your most important task when managing any information
gathering project is to produce the brief. Whether using
internal or external staff, the research will only be as good as
the brief given.

- Do not make the mistake of thinking your researcher is a
  mind-reader or has a crystal ball. Most are fairly ordinary
  people!
- If you do not explain what your want, you will not get it and
  researchers cannot forecast the future any more accurately
  than you, though they can provide you with information to
  help improve your forecasts.

Checklist for a research brief

- Background – tell the researcher about the business and the decisions which need to be made. Outline their significance and the information needs that you have.
- Provide the researcher with internal and external information sources that may help. Leaving them to find their own is *not* a test of their abilities but an expensive waste of resources. You will be charged for what you already know and it will strain the relationship between you.
- Provide the specifics of the information needs, including any constraints and parameters, such as how big a sample is needed (i.e. how accurate the results must be), the geographic spread needed, and any constraints of time, cost or security.
- Decide together how the agencies' performance will be assessed and what controls regarding quality, etc. are required.
- Decide in what format you want them to report and what the administrative arrangements are – for example, their point of contact, details for payment and so on.

 At the end of any project take time to debrief the agency and your team. Review not just the work but also the process to see how improvements in communication or feedback format might help in the future.

Review of the information

Information is a valuable resource. It is critical to the planner, but to be of benefit in winning competitive advantage it must be reliable and of the quantity and quality which allows management to use it effortlessly in its decision-making.

Despite the dramatic increase in information technology the management of information is still in its infancy. Efforts must be made early if managers are to have information which they need, rather than that which others want to give them. In too many organizations information provision is a subsidiary activity of the finance department and its format and availability does not always meet the expectations of the managers who use it.

Be a demanding customer of information. Decide what you need and ask for it – be pro-active rather than reactive as a customer of information.

Once information systems are established you are well placed to begin work on your plans. If your information is inadequate then take steps to improve it. You cannot do everything at once, but work on the 'need to know' list.

As you work through the remainder of this book and develop your own plans you will identify information gaps. Make a note of them on the following page and then take actions to fill them. If you are not pro-active about collecting information you will get to next year's plan with the same gaps. Get your team to keep similar lists and add 'Information Issues' to your monthly team meetings. Set priorities and monitor improvements as more and better information becomes available to you.

Form 1 An information shopping list

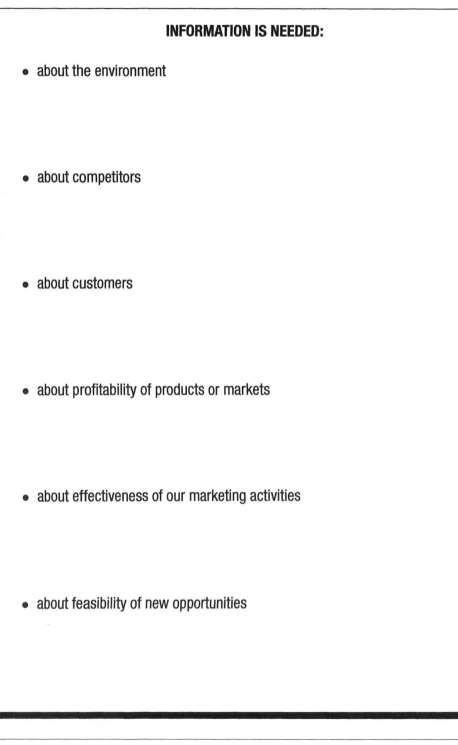

INFORMATION IS NEEDED:

- about the environment

- about competitors

- about customers

- about profitability of products or markets

- about effectiveness of our marketing activities

- about feasibility of new opportunities

CHAPTER 4

Measuring current market performance

Auditing the marketing activity

What constitutes the marketing activity?

The marketing outputs

Portfolio analysis

Customer analysis

Analyzing performance

Summary

Auditing the marketing activity

We saw in chapter 2 the overview of the planning sequence. It began with each of the functional activities analyzing their current position – undertaking an audit. In this chapter we will examine how that can be done for the marketing activity.

Measuring performance has not been something at which marketing professionals have historically been very good. We have shied away from setting quantified objectives and being held accountable for the resources we have spent. We have promoted marketing as an art rather than as a management science. As a result, when times were hard, management felt justified to cut the marketing budget. This was certainly understandable if not totally reasonable: if marketers cannot say what value they are adding, their actions cannot be supported.

That old approach is now pretty much a thing of the past. Marketing managers measure and control as effectively as any other function, and as more and more information is generated from feedback and controls so we learn even more to help us improve next year's effectiveness.

In this chapter we will consider what kind of analysis is available to help the marketer answer the question, 'Where are we now?' and complete Step 1 in the planning sequence. We will examine how to:

- analyze the product portfolio and customer segments
- assess distribution channels and measure promotional effectiveness
- benchmark customer care standards
- generate a checklist for your own promotional audit.

What constitutes the marketing activity?

There are two aspects to the marketing activities of an organization, the marketing processes and the output of those processes:

The inputs	The output – the marketing mix
• The marketing team	– Product
• Marketing research resources	– Price
• MKIS	– Promotion
• New product development systems	– Place
• Role and status of marketing in the company	– People
• Communication and influence with internal and external suppliers	– Physical evidence
	– Processes

The inputs

We naturally assume that marketing is responsible for the marketing output – the marketing mix. But you will notice that this is in fact the output of the whole operation. Marketing's task is to co-ordinate and influence decisions on product, price and availability; but the extent to which it will be successful depends on the status of marketing in the business, the systems for decision-making and the degree of customer orientation amongst colleagues and senior managers – the quality of your marketing inputs. An audit of these inputs is certainly a useful exercise. It will give you an insight into how the organization views marketing and the investment which has gone into its role.

Your marketing team needs to be represented at the most senior level in the organization if it is to influence the business decision-makers.

Even when an organization is genuinely customer-oriented and senior managers make all decisions in a way which reflects the users' interests they will still need a strong marketing team:

- Research will still be needed to keep two-way communication channels with the customer open.
- New product development activities will benefit from a champion to represent the customer's interests.
- Promotional activities will need to be co-ordinated and integrated with other elements of the marketing mix to ensure a consistent positioning.
- A marketing plan will still be needed to implement the customer-focused business strategy and to ensure effective segmentation.

eg

No results without top level commitment

The UK public services have been relatively recent converts to marketing. Schools, universities, hospitals and public libraries are all now actively seeking ways of ensuring user satisfaction, and many have appointed marketing managers or officers. Too often these roles are at middle management level with limited access to the key decision-makers. Controlling and influencing the marketing mix is almost impossible from that position. At best these marketers can control the promotional activities of the operation because that budget is usually in their hands. The result is an organization which mistakenly thinks it has adopted marketing but has simply re-packaged its traditional operational orientation.

Marketing staff need to be qualified or trained professionals. Without a solid grasp of the frameworks and concepts of marketing and competence in using the marketing tools, resources are likely to be wasted, business opportunities missed and organizational potential left unfulfilled. Whilst marketing is not a difficult subject to master, it is seldom undertaken effectively by enthusiastic amateurs. If you would expect a qualified finance person to look after your financial resources, use the same standards for those responsible for your customers.

Take time out to assess the marketing function of your operation. Is it well placed to lead the organization's strategy and represent adequately the needs of your customers? If not, identify changes necessary to improve its status and resources. One of the first tasks of many customer aware managers is to market marketing. Run workshops, provide briefings to senior staff, find case studies of how things are done differently elsewhere, and get senior colleagues to read this book. If you are an unqualified marketer find out how to become a qualified professional.

The marketing outputs

The marketing mix is the term usually used to cover those aspects of the business decisions made to influence customer demand. The original four Ps of this mix are:

- the *product*/service
- its *promotion*
- its availability – *place*
- its *price*.

Three more have been added to these in order to cover the elements of the offering related especially to the service sectors. But as service becomes an increasingly important element in customer choice across all sectors, so the extra three Ps of the service mix have become more universally applicable:

- *people* – the customer care
- *physical evidence* – the environment, literature, packaging, etc.
- *processes* – from enquiry and booking systems to after-sales service.

The marketing audit normally refers to establishing the strengths and weaknesses of the activity in these categories, but judged from the perspective of the customer. Putting yourself in the customer's shoes is an important skill for marketers. Your product may be the cheapest on the market, but if the customer perceives it to be expensive then that is what will influence his or her purchase decision. Empathy and market research are critical to this stage of the audit process.

Where are we now? – the products and markets

It is important to remember why the audit is being undertaken. Future strategies will be selected on the basis of what this analysis identifies as our strengths. Other opportunities will be rejected because they would expose our weaknesses. The implications of your evaluation are therefore significant, and this work must be undertaken thoroughly and seriously.

Portfolio analysis

Most organizations, however small, offer more than one service – for example, the window cleaner may do interiors and exteriors, clear gutters or clean paintwork, whilst large multinationals will have a portfolio of products numbered in thousands. A starting point for any planner is to identify which products you want to sell more of. (Note the word product will be used as a generic term which implies both products and services.) Which represent the most contribution to profit or make the least demands on a limited resource? Which contribute most to the organization's vision or mission?

Surprisingly few organizations are able to say how profitable different products or services are. Find out about your own business and do not confuse revenue with profit margin – high value sales are not always the most profitable.

Marketing strategy and tactics can directly influence the mix of products sold. The retailer choosing to highlight one brand rather than another through her merchandising is well aware of this, so it is vital that marketers take the time to identify the most profitable products *before* developing their strategies and tactics.

The right choice
If the window cleaner's analysis shows that cleaning internal windows was more profitable than cleaning outside windows he might implement a plan designed to sell this additional service to more of his customer base. If, however, the regular external window cleaning contracts were identified as the most attractive then a plan to attract new customers and expand the core customer base would be a better use of his marketing effort.

With only a handful of products, this process may be relatively straightforward, but portfolio analysis tools are needed to help those with larger ranges.

The product life cycle

The product life cycle (PLC) is one of the best known models of marketing. It is useful because it illustrates clearly that change is inevitable as an offering moves through its life in the market. Each of the stages of the cycle are characterized by different conditions of demand and supply. To get the best returns from a product at all times the manager must be able to change the marketing mix at the different stages. For example, a high price may be appropriate for a newly launched innovative product with few competitors. This 'skimming' strategy will generate high profits early in the product's life, but once challenged by competitors in the growth stage, prices will need to fall if market share is to be maintained. Similarly, promotional activities must change from awareness generating, through persuasion to reminder as the product matures.

One reason for portfolio analysis is to ensure that managers have located each product on its life cycle before strategies are developed for them – see Fig. 4.1.

Fig 4.1 Product life cycle of a generic product

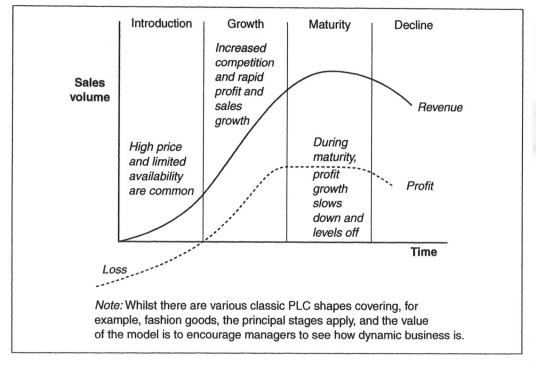

Note: Whilst there are various classic PLC shapes covering, for example, fashion goods, the principal stages apply, and the value of the model is to encourage managers to see how dynamic business is.

- Practising managers are sometimes quick to dismiss the 'theory' of management and marketing. This is a mistake because whilst it is important that you recognize their limitations the various tools and techniques can be of practical help. You need to add them to your personal toolbox so you can choose to use them when it suits you.
- Most tools and techniques have more than one application, and you can modify and adapt them, and choose to apply them or not, but do not dismiss them out of hand.

> **!!!**
>
> - One of the dangers with PLC is that managers take it too literally. If sales growth starts to slow down they assume that means the product is in transition from the growth phase to the maturity phase and modify their strategies and tactics accordingly. In fact, slower sales may be the result of a weak economy or competitive actions. The changing strategy will shorten the product's potential life unnecessarily – it becomes a self-fulfilling prophecy.
> - PLCs are useful indicators but should not be acted upon without thought and more evidence.

There are a number of practical limitations to the use of the product life cycle and some pitfalls to be avoided, but it does demonstrate the reason for developing a balanced portfolio and shows managers why products at the height of their revenue-generating life are not popular with the owners – because profit growth has levelled off. Most owners expect to see profit growth. To achieve that the business needs growing products or must find strategies for extending the life of already mature products – for example, boosting sales by opening up new markets, new distribution channels or modifying the existing product to encourage repeat purchases.

The Boston Matrix

The PLC can be used to track and forecast demand for a product, and compare brands within a generic product range, but is of less help when trying to evaluate an extensive and diverse portfolio. Management practitioners and academics have worked to produce a variety of tools to improve portfolio analysis.

Fig 4.2 The Boston Matrix

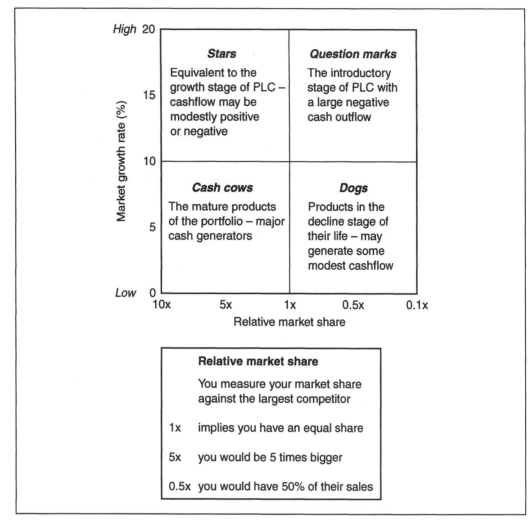

Consider the depiction of two organizations' portfolios using the Boston Matrix – see Fig. 4.3. The size of the circles indicates revenue generated by each business unit or product, and the arrow the direction each is moving in.

The Boston Matrix has its limitations, particularly for public sector players where market share and growth are not particularly relevant. For others, however, it can be a useful technique for getting a snapshot of all the products offered

Fig 4.3 Managing a portfolio

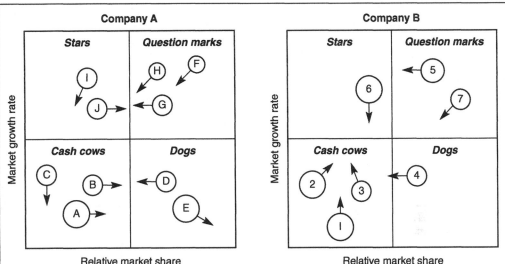

Company A is in the much less healthy position:

- it is trying to fund too many new and growing products, probably with insufficient resources to do everything successfully, and has made the mistake of spreading itself too thinly
- products A and B are rapidly becoming dogs, leaving only C and perhaps I as major cash generators
- the lack of investment in the stars may explain J reverting to a question mark
- dog E should probably be removed from the portfolio to release resources for the new products.

Company B is in a much stronger position:

- there are three good-sized cash generators, two of which are in growing markets
- there is a manageable number of new products, and the one dog is showing signs of becoming a cash generator again.

or the business units operating, and the likely financial implications for the business of the current portfolio balance.

Even if it is a 'back of the envelope' calculation, look at the products in your portfolio (or the strategic business units within your organization) using the grid in Fig. 4.4. What conclusions can you draw?

Fig 4.4 Boston Matrix grid

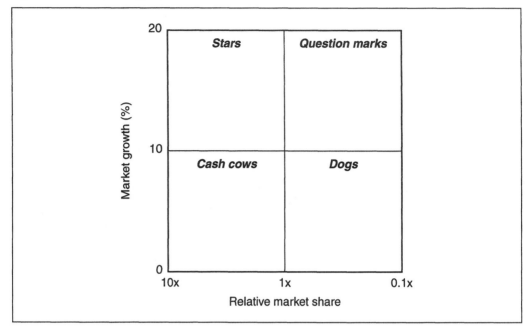

The GE or multi-factor matrix

This third tool of portfolio analysis is one of the most useful for any manager's toolbox. It can be used, as here, to analyze current products or, as we will see in later chapters, to help evaluate alternative strategies or new markets. One of its main attractions is its flexibility, which allows management teams to decide on variables relevant to their business or organization. This makes it as useful to not-for-profit organizations as private sector ones. It also means that a range of factors can be taken into account when you assess the portfolio – a much more realistic option.

The GE Matrix was developed by consultants McKinsey on behalf of General Electric and is sometimes referred to as the multi-factor portfolio model.

The concept of this technique is simple – it seeks to measure the attractiveness of a product or opportunity on two dimensions:

- its attractiveness to the company – *product attractiveness*. In other words its potential profit and/or revenue generation, fit with company policy and other products, and its growth forecasts, etc.
- its attractiveness to customers – *competitive advantage*. It looks at how likely customers are to buy this product by considering the customers' buying criteria in terms of price, performance, availability, etc., and provides a framework for the company to evaluate its likely performance against these criteria.

Locating your portfolio on the matrix – Fig. 4.5 – is also a relatively straightforward mapping activity. A number of computer programs now exist which will take the hard work out of the mechanical calculations for this exercise.

Fig 4.5 GE Matrix

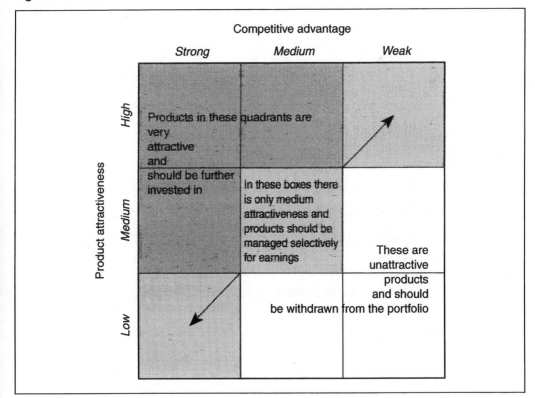

Using the GE Matrix

The management team get together to compile a list of the characteristics or criteria which they would use to judge an attractive product. Where possible add quantification:

Step 1
- profitable ✗   gross margin above 24 per cent ✓
- low risk ✗   chances of success in excess of 2:1 ✓
- a cash generator ✗   sales of at least £0.5m next year ✓

Make sure that any limiting factors like funding, machine time or a scarce resource are added as selection criteria.

Step 2
Once management's list is complete the various factors need to be weighted because some will be more important than others. Growth potential may be twice as important as current sales, for example. Managers can have as many factors as they want in their list, but the total weight which can be given to the list is 10. It is easier until you get used to the concept to keep the number of criteria limited to 10 or fewer.

You should now have an agreed and weighted list of product attractiveness criteria – see Fig. 4.6.

If your company has never used this technique you will find a facilitator very helpful in getting consensus and agreement. This could be a consultant or an internal colleague. You will find considerable and often heated debates about the importance of profit growth against short-term revenue, risk vs investment, etc. Even as a stand-alone exercise for team communication this activity cannot be recommended too strongly.

Fig 4.6 Product attractiveness

• Sales ↑ £0.5m	2.0
• Growth forecasts ↑ 5% per annum	3.0
• Close synergy with other products	1.0
• Purchases insensitive to price	0.5
• High tendency for cross selling	1.5
• Low investment needs ↓ £0.2m	0.25
• Low demands on manufacturing capacity	1.75
	10.0

However many criteria in your list, the total weighting allocated must equal 10.

Step 3

You now take each product in your portfolio and score it (0–5) on its performance against these criteria. Product A might score highly on sales revenue (5) because it's earning £1m a year but low on growth (1) as the forecast is for a market reduction of 2 per cent next year. Product B on the other hand may do well on synergy with other products (4) but needs a lot of investment next year and so only gets (2) for that rating – see Fig. 4.7.

Step 4

Once *all* your products have been scored you can now calculate a total for each by multiplying the rating score by the weighting allocated for each criterion and then totalling them. The maximum possible score is 50: if each criterion (total weighted value of 10) scored the maximum of 5 (5 × 10 = 50) and the lowest a 0 if a product received a zero score against each of the criteria – see Fig. 4.8.

You now have a quantified measure of product attractiveness for each of your potential products. The criteria and their relative importance have been kept constant for each, ensuring some element of objectivity in the team's evaluation. The assessment is transparent and reasons for a relatively low score can be identified and if necessary tackled or reviewed – for example, product A scored badly on growth yet this is given a weighting of 3 by the organization.

Fig 4.7 Product scoring (0-5)

Criteria	Product A	Product B
Sales	5	3
Growth	1	3
Synergy	3	4
Price sensitivity	4	4
Cross sell	2	3
Investment	1	2
Capacity needs	3	3

Rate each product on a 0–5 score against the set criteria

Fig 4.8 Relative attractiveness of options

Criteria	Weighting	Product A Score × (0 – 5)	Product A Total weighted score	Product B Score × (0 – 5)	Product B Total weighted score
Sales	2.0	5	10.0	3	6.0
Growth	3.0	1	3.0	3	9.0
Synergy	1.0	3	3.0	4	3.0
Price sensitivity	0.5	4	2.0	4	2.0
Cross sell	1.5	2	3.0	3	4.5
Investment	0.25	1	0.25	2	0.5
Capacity needs	1.75	3	5.25	3	5.25
			26.5		30.25

Step 5

A similar process is now required to generate a score of competitive advantage: the customer's assessment of each product's relative attractiveness – a measure of its strengths.

To be a true reflection of the customer's views this really requires market research, but management may be able to get some measure of competitive advantage by substituting its own judgements.

A weighted list of the customer's criteria for selecting a product in this market needs to be established. Again the number of criteria does not matter, but the total allocation of weighting must equal 10 – see Fig. 4.9.

Step 6

The performance of each product in your portfolio needs to be scored against these criteria (0–5) and those scores multiplied by the weightings to give you a total out of 50, representing the competitive advantage of each product – see Fig. 4.10.

Fig 4.9 Using customer criteria

Criteria	Weighting	Again, qualification
Price	1.0	against an industry
Performance	3.0	benchmark
Availability	2.0	will help
After sales	3.5	the scoring later
Reputation	0.5	
	10.0	

Fig 4.10 Comparing advantages

Criteria	Weighting ×	Product A Value (0 – 5)	Product A Total weighted score	Product B Value × (0 – 5)	Product B Total weighted score
Price	1.0	1	1.0	3	3.0
Performance	3.0	2	6.0	4	12.0
Availability	2.0	1	2.0	3	6.0
After sales	3.5	2	7.0	4	14.0
Reputation	0.5	3	1.5	4	2.0
	10.0		17.5		37.0

Each product should now have a second score out of 50, representing a measure of the customer's view of its attractiveness or competitive advantage.

Whereas the criteria and weighting were constant for the manager's view to ensure objectivity, different customer groups may have different buying priorities. You may need to modify your criteria and weighting across the portfolio. Remember that you are simply looking for an opportunity where you can perform well.

Step 7

The final step in the process is to log each product on to the matrix using the two scores to establish its position – see Fig. 4.11. The size of the circle is used to illustrate current revenue from each.

Analysis

Product B is worth increased investment and development – the customers like it and it is a relatively attractive product to the company. Product A, however, is close to being a candidate

Fig 4.11 Plotting product attractiveness

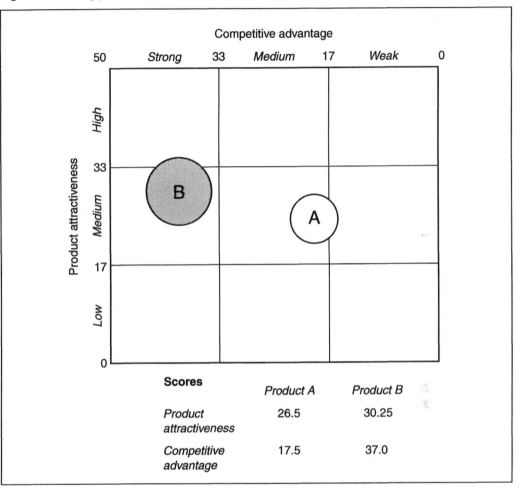

Scores	Product A	Product B
Product attractiveness	26.5	30.25
Competitive advantage	17.5	37.0

for withdrawal. It is not popular with company or client, its future needs to be considered and certainly it needs managing for cashflow. Further investment should only be considered if significant repositioning of the product is possible.

- Because the principles of this matrix model are so versatile you will find it very adaptable and particularly useful for strategic evaluation and decision-making.
- If you were not already familiar with the matrix, try to practise using it and you will find it a useful addition to your management toolbox.

Customer analysis

The fact that your products were targeted at a particular segment of the market does not necessarily mean that they are in fact, or should be, your target customers. Audit time is a good opportunity to assess your market and customers:

- What market are you in?
- Who are your current customers?
- Who is involved in the purchase decision?
- What motivates their behaviour?
- Which customers are worth most?

If you have an effective marketing information system and a history of marketing research behind you, much of this will already be known, but if not you will need to take actions to find out.

What market are you in?

You are trying to build a map of your market. This map will provide you with a focus for all your planning activities, defining competitors, customers and channels to market. You can add as much or as little detail to your map as you want or have information for. The market share of competitors, the percentage of product or service through a particular channel to market and purchase motivations can all be usefully added, if known, to build a picture of the business.

To begin your own market map you must clarify what business is done from the customers' perspective – it is the customer who decides who your competitors are. The local cinema should not necessarily assume that its competitors are other cinemas in the region. More likely, the local theatre, restaurants and even the video hire shop will represent the real competitors for scarce leisure time and entertainment spend. It is always worth remembering that 'Do it yourself' is often a very viable alternative to your offering and should be considered as a competitor. Trends and developments which facilitate DIY can then be monitored and reacted to.

Even from the simple map shown in Fig. 4.12 you can see that only B and C compete for retail business in segments 4 and 1. Both A and C have direct sell operations but currently focus on different market segments.

Fig 4.12 Market mapping

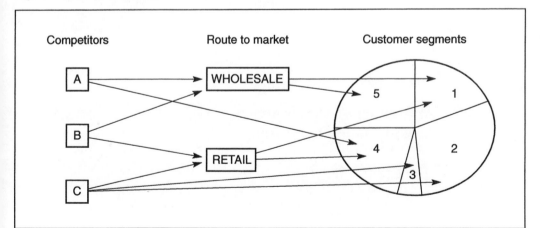

Developing a map can often be done from general knowledge of the marketplace, but can produce useful insights and help managers identify opportunities and competitive threats.

Malcolm McDonald and Ian Dunbar's book, *Market Segmentation* (Macmillan, 1995), provides a detailed approach for market mapping.

Who are your customers?

Profile your current customer base to identify which segments of the market they come from and identify any common characteristics and buying behaviour patterns which might help future segmentation or marketing tactics.

- Do not limit yourself to geo-demographic characteristics like age, sex, location, company size, etc. but look for behavioural similarities – why do they buy, when and from whom?
- A keen amateur gardener aged 25 may have more in common with a fellow enthusiast aged 65 than with others in his or her own age group. Their common interest might influence the books and magazines they read, the TV programmes they watch, as well as the selection of purchases made with their discretionary income.

Who influences the decision?

Asking who your customers are is easy. The answers are frequently much more complex. Research may be needed to establish precisely who is in your decision-making unit (DMU). Depending on the characteristics of the product and the circumstances of its purchase there may be one or many involved.

Using Fig. 4.13, can you identify those who make up your DMU?

Fig 4.13 The decision-making unit

Elements of DMU	Role	Your DMU
Starter or trigger	The person or event which prompts a purchase	
Purchaser	The individual who takes legal title of the product – the customer	
Adviser	Anyone who advises or influences the purchaser – a retailer, friend or editorial recommendation	
Decider	The person or persons who make the final decisions on brand/supplier, etc. – it may or may not include the purchaser	
End-user	The consumer – the person who uses up the product or service	
Financier	The budget holder	

It may be quite difficult to research the DMU in your industry. For those selling to the public sector or large companies it can be very time consuming to identify those who will make up the decision-making committee and even harder to establish their relative influence and importance.

Relationship marketing requires that the sales organization penetrates the client company much more effectively, getting behind the buyer to build relationships with the whole of the DMU. In this way a much more stable relationship based on a partnership of problem solving can be established.

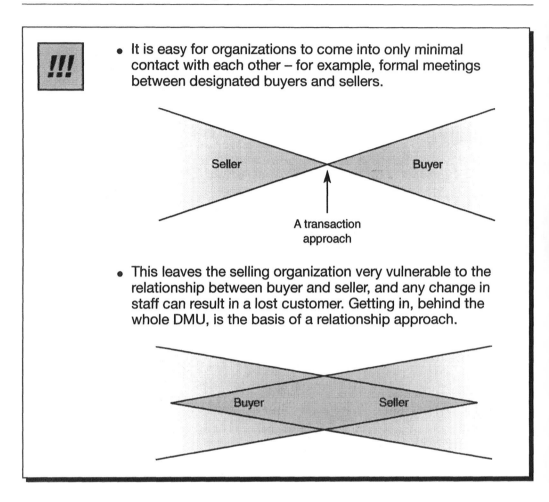

- It is easy for organizations to come into only minimal contact with each other – for example, formal meetings between designated buyers and sellers.

- This leaves the selling organization very vulnerable to the relationship between buyer and seller, and any change in staff can result in a lost customer. Getting in, behind the whole DMU, is the basis of a relationship approach.

What motivates customer behaviour?

Understanding motivation and buyer behaviour is the key to successful marketing activity. You *must* know the needs of all those operating as part of the DMU.

Customers only buy products and services to solve problems; the *benefits* you offer must directly address their needs.

eg	**What is the real motivator?** The business executive charged with choosing a new computer system may not *need* a no-glare screen or user-friendly operating system. They are the features which offer benefits to the end-user. The executive may be a low-risk purchaser – a person valuing reliability and reputation. He or she does not want the responsibility and stain on his or her record of a poor purchase decision. IBM recognized this need amongst executive deciders and ran very successfully its campaign with the strapline, 'no one was ever fired for choosing IBM'.

The essence of a marketing approach to business is simple:

- identify customer needs/motives
- use your skills to produce product or service features which address those needs
- promote the benefits of those features to the targeted segment.

Research is essential to identify the real motives of customers' behaviour. You need answers to the questions, why do they buy or not buy? And why do they choose this brand or colour? This requires qualitative/motivational research as we discussed in chapter 3.

This type of research frequently produces interesting results. Time after time organizations find that what they are selling is not what the customer is buying:

- the doctor issues prescriptions to the patient who wanted reassurance
- the dry cleaner prides himself on the sharpness of the creases and finish of his garments but the customers chose him because of the convenience of a nearby car park
- the chef offers the freshest ingredients to diners who chose the restaurant because of its atmosphere.

It is vital to know what factors are really motivating your customers' behaviour so resources are invested in providing benefits which the customer values.

---

eg   **Just in time advantage**
Many companies have found themselves investing heavily to be able to offer just in time (JIT) availability. Better logistics and relocated distribution centres may have cut delivery times down significantly, but this will only win more customers if faster response times matter to the client. Those whose systems mean they can always order a week in advance will use the 24-hour system, but it will not influence their purchase decisions and they will not be prepared to pay a premium price for it.

Customer orientation means giving customers what they want and value, not what you *think* they want.

Total product concept
The total bundle of benefits offered to the customer is described by Philip Kotler as the total product concept. This concept identifies some benefits which are core or expected by the customer and others which augment or differentiate one company's offering from another. To have any impact on customer behaviour the benefits offered must be valued by the customer.

If all the organizations offer the same benefits, purchase decisions will be based on price and the market will commoditize.

Successful operators offer the necessary core and expected benefits but then differentiate their offer with augmented elements of the package which research has shown are important to the customers – faster delivery, longer operating hours or more attractive packaging. Any elements of the marketing mix can be employed to differentiate and avoid customers buying on price alone.

What are your customers worth?

It is unlikely that all your customers are equally profitable or valuable to you. In practice the Pareto Principle (the 80:20 rule) often holds true – 80 per cent of your business revenue or profits comes from just 20 per cent of your customers. Review your results to see if this is true for you. Once identified, you can work to attract more similar users, build stronger relationships with this 20 per cent and seek to grow business from the others.

You may also find 80 per cent of your limiting factors, perhaps your time and management effort, goes on 20 per cent of the customers. Identify them and you can consider de-marketing to this group. This may reduce demand and release resources for more productive uses – another way of getting more from less.

- It is easy to be seduced by bigger accounts – to celebrate winning that large order – but bigger customers may demand special attention, bigger discounts and preferential after sales service. They are not always the most profitable.
- On the other hand lots of small accounts may raise the servicing costs. Either way the segments you choose to target are likely to impact on the profitability of your activities. Know which you want to target before producing your marketing strategy.

Remember when you consider the value of a customer not to think just about the transaction but also about the lifetime value of a relationship with you. The customer's propensity to remain loyal and to buy other products from your portfolio should also get consideration.

Your current customer base can be analyzed to help you identify targets for market penetration. If you plot key clients or customer categories in terms of their average value and the estimated percentage of their potential spend this shows how you can identify the most attractive targets – see Fig. 4.14.

Fig 4.14 Evaluating your customer base

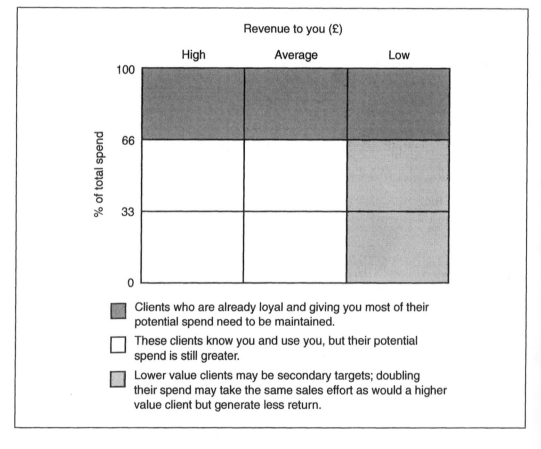

Word of warning

A small company should take care when considering growing business from an already high value client. They need to take care not to become too dependent on one customer and change the balance of power between them and the key account.

Strengths and weaknesses of the mix

Once your analysis has identified the profitability of your customers and various products, you can move on to the audit of your marketing mix. Every dimension of the offering needs to be examined from the customer's perspective and viewed relative to the closest competitor's offering.

An audit checklist

Use the following checklist – see Fig. 4.15 – as a template for undertaking an audit of your own operation, or one with which you are familiar. Add to or amend the list to suit your business. If you haven't completed an audit recently try one now. What do your results tell you? Remember to keep a list of those information gaps.

- Add numbers or weighting wherever possible. It adds much more meaning and relevance to your audit. Do not ask whether customer care is good or bad, but rather ask how you would rate customer care on a scale of +10 to –10.
- Even better is to break this down into constituent parts, such as how friendly/approachable you would rate your staff or how rapidly you responded to a customer's enquiry.
- Once you have completed your audit in this way it can be used as a part of your control mechanisms, with this year's analysis useful as a benchmark of performance for next year.

Fig 4.15 Audit checklist

	+10	0	−10
	Strengths	*Weaknesses*	

	Strengths	Weaknesses
Product • technical excellence • reputation • functionality • performance • reliability • running costs • •		
Price • competitiveness • terms of payment • discounts • loyalty discounts • special offers • •		
Promotion • image • level of awareness • personal contact with sales • 'brand identity' • •		

Fig 4.15 Continued

	+10	0 Strengths	−10 Weaknesses
Place • space capacity • seasonality of demand • last-minute availability • booking systems • location • •			
People • customer care • technical skills • motivation/flexibility • relationships • talent • •			
Processes • booking systems • service system • quality assurance • after-sales follow-up • •			
Physical evidence • brochures • uniforms • business environment • packaging • •			

Marketing strategists make decisions which impact directly on the gross profitability of the business. Changes in:

- the mix of products
- the mix of customers
- the spend on the marketing mix

are all the drivers of gross profit. It is therefore critical that what is and is not profitable/desirable business is clarified before plans are laid.

Analyzing performance

Numbers and quantification are key to planning. A detailed audit requires more than just a review of customer perceptions – you need to find out what works and what does not. The feedback information set-up for the implementation of this year's plan should provide you with a flow of information for this stage of the auditing process.

If you have not got this information available to you, add it to our information shopping list in chapter 3 and make a point of collecting it in the future.

Two areas are of particular importance – distribution and promotion – because both are very expensive aspects of the business activities. You must be able to assess the performance in both areas.

Distribution

What element of the final price represents distribution costs? It is often as much as 50 per cent. Savings here represent large percentage improvements in profitability and are to a great extent driving the push towards direct sell.

If you are using intermediaries you need to be able to evaluate their performance. Measure and compare them on:

- sales
- cost of servicing
- quality of service
- product knowledge of their staff
- provision of additional support services
- co-operation with promotional initiatives
- access to end-user information.

Your review should cover both qualitative and quantitative aspects of their performance.

The multi-factor matrix can be very successfully modified both to evaluate existing channels and to help you to select new ones. Criteria for assessing *channel attractiveness* must be selected and weighted, and your channels evaluated against this. The competitive advantage dimension is a measure of how likely it is that the channel will want to do business with you. You must note that they are not interested in the product but the business opportunity it represents. Giving you 'shelf space' will be judged against margins, promotional support, training, status, exclusivity, delivery service and trade incentives. Research is needed to determine which of these matters to your channels, and your performance must then be rated against them.

Promotion

The lion's share of any sales and marketing budget will go on promotional activity. It is vital that marketers are able to measure the effectiveness of their spending. Feedback and analysis of results are the foundation stones for improving tomorrow's performance.

Do not try to judge the effectiveness of advertising by the increase in sales. Advertising impacts on awareness and, to a lesser extent, on attitude, but seldom does it directly 'shift' product.

To analyze promotion properly you need to appreciate the decision-making process (DMP).

Unaware   Aware   Interest   Desire   Action

Customers have to be shifted through the stages from unawareness to action. Some of the communication tools are better at some tasks in this process than others. Advertising, publicity and exhibitions work strongly at generating awareness and interest, whilst point of sale, sales promotion and personal selling are strongest at generating action. To audit what parts of your communication activity need attention you need to research current levels of awareness and attitudes as well as sales.

Using ratios

Colleagues in the finance department will have a whole checklist of financial ratios which they use to help audit the financial health of the operation. Ratios are excellent tools of control as they can be used for comparisons and benchmarking. Marketers must learn not to be afraid of these quantitative tools and they can be of great help in analyzing promotional spend.

- Do not try to make decisions on the basis of one ratio. You need to have a basis for comparison, such as this year against last, this salesperson against another, and our performance against a competitor's.
- Do not jump to conclusions. One sales person's performance may be poorer than another because of environmental variations, not sales ability.

The ratios which are most useful to your business may be different, but consider the list below and add your own to it and see if you have information to allow you to calculate the following:

- Enquiries: sales
- Sales calls: orders
- Incremental sales: incremental promotional spend
- Selling costs: sales
- Operating profit: total marketing spend
- Sales expenses: sales
-
-
-

Let ratio analysis increase your insight of what might be happening – it will prompt you to ask questions and so improve your allocation of scarce promotional pounds.

Promotional effectiveness

As with all planning, promotional planning is about using scarce resources efficiently and effectively – see Fig. 4.16.

Effective marketing, relevant segmentation and appropriate positioning will ensure that promotional messages are targeted and relevant to the intended audience. Efficient promotion is dependent on the communication skills of the manager, integrating and co-ordinating messages to ensure they are delivered in the most cost-effective way.

Fig 4.16 Promotional effectiveness grid

	Effective	Ineffective
Efficient	The right messages to the right audience at the lowest promotional cost	Low promotional budget, but the message not received by the right people
Inefficient	The right messages received by the right people, but at an unnecessarily high promotional cost	High spend and the wrong message!

Summary

The activities necessary to audit your marketing performance and activities thoroughly are extensive if you start from scratch, but as your information and feedback flows improve so the task becomes more routine. Do not worry if there are gaps in your audit to start with. Begin the process with what is available to you and develop more depth and sophistication as your planning experience and systems evolve.

Once you have completed your audit and analysis you can sort your information to provide:

- senior management with a snapshot of the marketing activity – as an input to the situational audit
- the marketing team with an *aide-mémoire* for reference when developing their strategies.

It can also be used:

- as the basis of a priority checklist for areas of activity which require attention and improvement
- as the benchmark for monitoring performance changes year on year.

Fig 4.17 Improving on your strengths

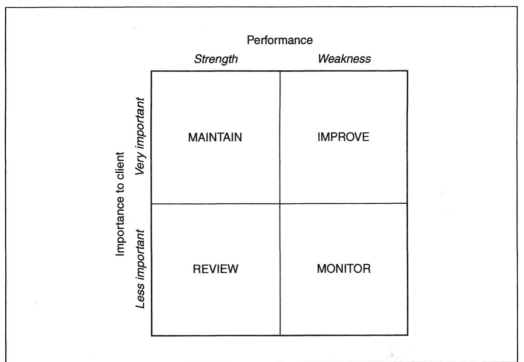

This chapter has dealt only with issues related to auditing the marketing activity, but as indicated in chapter 2 this first step in the business planning process would also be taking place across all functional areas. These assessments combined represent the overall situational analysis.

 Don't let the lack of information stop you moving forward with planning. Make assumptions and use controls to check their eventual validity. Plan to fill information gaps over time.

CHAPTER 5

Ensuring the external focus

The role of the environmental audit

The significance of environmental monitoring

Gathering environment intelligence

Environmental factors

About the competition

Contingency and scenario plans

Using the environmental audit

The role of the environmental audit

Neither organizations nor their customers exist in a vacuum. Both are part of and influenced by a rapidly changing external environment. Business strategy cannot be developed without reference to this environment because the fortunes of the operation will be determined by environmental factors. Too many managers have in the past kept their heads in the sand, waiting until environmental change happened before reacting to it. Increasingly businesses recognize that there are significant commercial advantages in being proactive in their strategies. Speed can generate competitive advantage in fast moving markets.

In this chapter we will examine the way in which marketing can help a business by providing this external focus. We will consider:

- the significance of environmental monitoring
- sources of market intelligence
- competitor analysis
- the role of scenario and contingency planning.

The significance of environmental monitoring

Effective plans cannot be produced in isolation but must be established in a way which exploits emerging opportunities and responds to any emerging threats. Opportunities and threats come about because of changes in the external environment. A manager's task is made more difficult because of the speed at which change can occur. Advance warning systems, a sophisticated intelligence gathering mechanism and contingency plans enabling rapid reaction are essential to all organizations successfully operating in today's demanding markets. Across public and private sectors the extent of change in any 5-10 year period (i.e. the lifetime of a long-term business plan) is awesome.

---

eg

Competing for students
In the education sector in the UK schools and colleges now have increased opportunities to compete for students. Success attracts additional resources, which was not the case in the past. Staff have had to accept new conditions of service, and budget cuts have forced reorganization and new methods of working. Technology has introduced new innovations in learning and potential new competitors, whilst social changes have influenced what people want to learn and how they will learn. User expectations have been raised, and for educational establishments to survive they must be able to respond quickly and creatively. What about your sector – what have been the key changes in your area and what is still on the cards?

Gathering environment intelligence

Depending on the size and nature of your business, this can be a large-scale formal activity or a smaller, relatively informal, one. Much intelligence can be gathered simply by keeping your ears and eyes open.

A small local trader can see the new housing development and be prepared to target residents as they move in. Local statistics on employment, economic growth and development projects will be reported by the local media – many will have a potential impact on the local business.

For larger operations a more formalized approach to environmental auditing will help to establish a flow of useful data and mean little additional activity is necessary when it comes around to producing the business plan.

The problem with environmental information is the sheer amount of data that can be collected. To prevent managers disappearing under a deluge of paper, decisions need to be taken about what external information might be important to the organization and then to identify sources or indicators which could be used to monitor that factor.

!!! Whilst some changes, like population movements, are normally long-term and can be monitored periodically and forecast well in advance, others like technological breakthroughs can occur at any time. Deciding that March is the month for looking at your environment runs the risk of you not identifying an event which happened in November. Ad hoc approaches to the external environment need to be replaced by mechanisms for continuous monitoring to avoid this pitfall. For example, if as a trader you use the weekly local paper for intelligence, scan it weekly not just occasionally.

Using census information
The census is a good example of secondary data easily available to local and national organizations. A nursery school wanting to develop a five-year plan needs census information to help forecast intake in five years' time. It does not, however, need all the information on deaths and marriages, only the local birth rate data and trends. A school which takes in pupils at 11 and is trying to produce its plan will find an easier source of intelligence is to monitor the fluctuation in places at the nursery school.

Environmental factors

The environmental factors which all organizations need to monitor can be categorized under the following headings:

- political and legal
- economic and demographic
- social and cultural
- technological.

The first step in establishing an auditing system is to brainstorm the influences under each heading that might impact on your business. Figure 5.1 (overleaf) is an example of the list which might be drawn up by a large building company.

Over time Constructit could refine and add to this list, but this gives them a starting point. The next step is to decide how best to monitor factors on the list – see Fig. 5.2.

Once this list has been established, a timetable of actions and responsibilities can be drawn up. One manager might be responsible for legal and political issues and so undertake the daily scanning of the press, taking and circulating relevant cuttings, attending workshops or briefings and then reporting back to colleagues. Someone else may look after technical buildings issues and concentrate on the trade press and attend annual exhibitions. An office assistant may be interested in design and changing fashions which influence customer expectations and so may monitor the general media for interesting articles and trends. By splitting the responsibilities up, more people in the team will become externally focused. The overall task and responsibility is shared and the process normalized and automatically built into the decision-making process.

Take the time to visit your main library and, if relevant, your trade or local business library. Familiarize yourself with the data available there, such as the surveys published by governments and professional bodies, user groups and pressure groups. You will probably be surprised at how much material is readily available. Similarly, talk to the local Chamber of Commerce to establish local information services and what they contain.

Fig 5.1 A macro-environmental audit summary for Constructit Builders

Political and legal	*Economic and demographic*
• changes in national or local regulations on building land and its uses/appeals	• movements in house prices
• health and safety legislation	• changing availability of housing finance
• political moves to influence home ownership	• population shifts – north to south, rural to urban, etc.
• changes in contract law influencing liability or indemnity	• average income levels
• legal changes influencing building materials and methods, e.g. asbestos ban	• taxation levels and mortgage interest relief
	• family size patterns
Social and cultural	*Technological*
• buyers' attitudes to home ownership	• methods of building
• changes in family life patterns – early/later marriage, more single families, etc.	• improvements in insulation/solar heating, etc.
• demand for different facilities due to increased at-home leisure activities	• equipment expectations – computerization of home management systems, easy maintenance kitchens
• expectations of what constitutes a 'good' property, e.g. garden size	

Fig 5.2 Monitoring environmental factors

Issue	Source	Frequency
building methods technology	– trade press – trade exhibitions	– monthly – 2 per annum
buyer expectations	– general research surveys – magazines and media programmes on living/homes, etc.	– library search for quarterly trade and reports – weekly programme review – monthly review of key titles
building legislation changes	– national press – trade association	– daily – regular contact

A note on international markets

If you are involved in developing business internationally then the environmental auditing activity becomes even more vital. You start with a basic appreciation of your own environment – everything from weather patterns to cultural expectations are instinctive. In international markets this is not the case. Simply comparing data may not be enough to give you a realistic picture either. Average income levels for India and Malaysia are meaningless unless you have a sense of standards of living, price levels, family structure and cultural expectations. Cultural differences are the most difficult to recognize and yet, because of their importance in influencing buyer behaviour, they are critical to the business planner.

You cannot understand the needs of your overseas clients if you do not meet them and get to know them. Secondary data alone is inadequate, and field research is essential, local partners and strategic alliances are often very effective ways of ensuring that companies have this local market understanding.

About the competition

The final element in the environmental audit is the competition. Who are they, and what is their strategy? Here intelligence gathering can quickly become unethical or downright illegal, and the management team should first clarify the parameters of what is acceptable behaviour. In the early 1990s British Airways was embarassed to find over-zealous managers had tapped into the computer systems of competitor Virgin Airlines, and industrial espionage is not uncommon in many industries. Inviting key employees from rival firms to apply for a fictitious post is a less aggressive common technique, but other methods of getting to know your competitors and forecasting their market behaviour may be more appropriate for you. You may be surprised to find just how many sources of information are available to you.

A checklist of competitor intelligence sources

- Sales teams and distributors who are out in the field will often have direct contact with competitors' representatives and will be the first to know of changes, new product launches, higher than expected sales bonuses and so on.
- Trade and industry gatherings, exhibitions, conferences and social events are ideal opportunities to pick up titbits of information.
- The trade press will often provide insight into the business plans and problems of competitors.
- Your customers may have direct experience of your competitors. They will be well placed to comment on the variations of performance, why they chose you and the reason others might prefer the competitors.

- Mystery shopping allows you or your team to step directly into the shoes of the customer. This is an excellent method of monitoring your own customer care as well as theirs. You can send for brochures, ask for demonstrations or quotes, and compare service levels. Purchases of competitors' goods allow detailed analysis of performance and components to benchmark against your own product or service standards.
- Annual reports and promotional material are unlikely to give much away but are sometimes surprisingly frank. They will give broad indicators of performance, which might be a useful insight, though creative financial manipulation of the figures means you need to be wary as to how reliable this information is.

- As with the other aspects of the environment you need to establish mechanisms for catching all competitor intelligence. Gossip heard by a sales rep may have little meaning to him or her, but reported to the business planner may have a lot of significance.
- Feedback opportunities at regular sales meetings, on sales call sheets and debrief sessions after industry events are the sort of systems which will help you keep up to date with competitor activity.
- Allocate a key competitor to each member of your management team and expect them to be the competitor watcher. Spreading the load encourages depth of analysis, and regular debriefs and presentations keep the whole team up to date.

Competitor strategy

Why do companies have to worry so much about competitors? Life would certainly be easier if you could simply develop a strategy and get on with implementing it. But this is not a very realistic approach.

- Business is very much like a game, with analogies and planning terminology common to both.
- We speak of a 'level playing field', meaning all the competitors are treated equally, have access to the same opportunities and so on.
- The football manager knows that his selected strategies must play to the strengths of his team but also exploit the weaknesses of the opposition.
- His game plan may need to be revised because of a substitution, unexpected weather conditions or in light of the performance after the first half.

Competitors in business are also likely to impact on your performance. It is possible for both companies to emerge as winners in some scenarios – for example, in a rapidly growing market. In these circumstances co-operation and collaboration may be a preferred strategy. In the main, however, you are both likely to be battling for the same customers and a bigger share of a mature or perhaps declining market. There will be winners and losers and the competition can be fierce.

Avoiding head-to-head competition

Knowing the competition well allows you to operate in the same market while minimizing head-to-head competition. Price wars, promotional duels and distribution conflicts are the evidence of companies locking horns. The strongest will emerge victorious but often weakened. The loser may even fail to survive. Customers may gain short-term benefits as they are aggressively wooed by the protagonists – seduced by special offers and cheaper prices – but in the long term the reduced choice and reduction in competition within the sector will probably work against customer interests.

Strategic marketing planning reduces this wasteful competitive activity. The process of segmentation means two companies can operate in the same market without competing directly for the same customers. By differentiating their offerings to meet the specific needs of their target, each can be the preferred supplier to its own customers – see Fig. 5.3.

A and B are in the hotel business, but the guests who prefer the traditional image and four-star service of A never seriously consider the modern three-star alternative offered by B. Both can operate without direct competition as long as their segment of customers remains large enough to satisfy their own objectives.

If customers leave their segment for whatever reason, or if either firm wants to expand, then competition, at first at the margins for floating customers, and later more directly for market share, might develop.

Direct competition is always an expensive activity and co-operation should always be considered as an alternative. For example, working together, both hotels A and B may be able to attract more people to the town – growing the total market.

Fig 5.3 Positioning the offering

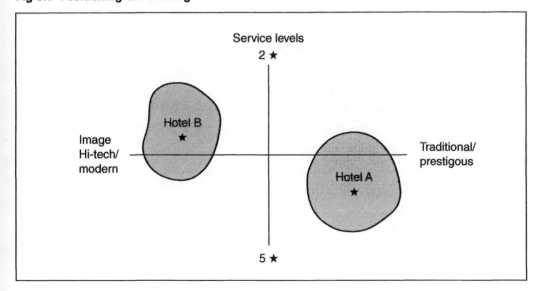

Firms also must be clear who their competitors really are. This process begins by defining the business you are in.

Research may reveal that firms within the same industry are not your main competitors, but another sector is competing for the disposable income of your customers. For example, charities in the UK have found themselves competing directly with the National Lottery. Your local theatre is competing with restaurants and the cinema to offer you a night out.

Influences on competitive activity

The size and number of firms which make up an industry will determine the nature of competitive activity. The monopolist has no direct competition and will adopt strategies to prevent entrants to the sector by reinforcing barriers to entry. The greatest threat is likely to be from substitute products and the major opportunity lies in growing the market.

A sector like hairdressing or restaurants has large numbers of small competitors. The actions of one player are unlikely to impact significantly on others, so most will seek to differentiate their services, appealing to a small group of regular customers.

Once firms begin to expand and grow in size, so their strategies become of greater significance to their competitors. Large oligopolistic players – industries made up of between 2 and 12 large firms – like the retail banks, petrol companies and supermarkets, have to monitor competitor activity diligently. Each is strong enough to impact on the others, winning customers and market share through a creative change of strategy. The strategies of these players will be influenced by their pecking order. Market leaders tend to adopt defensive strategies, whilst market challengers are more aggressive in their approach. These firms, particularly in mature industries with little overall market growth, are most likely to fall into the trap of head-to-head battles for market share.

The firm, whether large or small, needs to identify carefully its closest competitors. Not necessarily the biggest, or the operation with the highest profile, but the companies that customers perceive to be competitors. Once identified, a response profile should be developed, requiring not simply an assessment of current strengths, weaknesses and capabilities but also a sense of the aspirations and goals of the firm in that marketplace.

If your closest competitor only gets 2 per cent of its business in this market his response to the competitive activities of your company may be much less vigorous than if 60 per cent of profits are dependent on this element of activity.

Porter's five forces

Management writer Michael Porter identified five forces, including the nature of competitive activity, which impact on a firm's potential performance. Changes in these forces are factors which the environmental audit should identify:

- the nature of competitive activity
- the threat of new entrants
- the threat of substitute products
- the power of suppliers
- the power of buyers.

Changes in the five forces indicate likely alterations in gross profit margins and a hardening or slackening of competitive pressures.

 Ask yourself, which of these five forces are changing in your business? What are the implications for your sales and profitability? What strategies might you adopt to minimize their impact?

Benefits of customer focus

Firms and organizations that develop the mechanisms to establish their external focus will be naturally customer-facing and are likely to be the first to identify marketplace changes, enabling them to respond pro-actively to both opportunities and threats. Those who insist on being inward-looking, with their backs to the customer, will continue to be taken by surprise by market developments. Their management will become adept firefighters and crisis managers.

At best they can hope to react quickly enough to survive until the next market shock. This is the team that is too busy dealing with today's emergency to find the time to undertake the important task of planning for tomorrow's business.

Contingency and scenario plans

No matter how good your environmental monitoring, there is always the possibility of the unexpected happening – freak weather, political unrest, natural or man-made disasters, an unexpected change in government or the collapse of a currency. Some events can be anticipated. The ending of apartheid in South Africa had been a possibility for years, but the speed with which change occurred was more unexpected. More of a surprise were the transition of Eastern European countries to market economies and the economic crisis in Asia during the late 1990s. Managers can be somewhat prepared for these less certain or unexpected events by developing contingency and scenario plans.

Contingencies are in place to cope with a possible rather than likely event. For example, you plan a party in the garden but have a contingency plan in case the weather is bad. All organizations should have contingency plans to prepare for things from a change of government, the arrival or departure of a competitor, to the collapse of a supply source.

Scenario plans are less likely events; they are 'what if?' plans. You may have one in case you win the lottery. Scenario planning has its advantages:

- encouraging managers to look creatively at the way in which environment influences strategy
- giving the opportunity for managers to develop and practise planning skills
- creating the opportunity for a competitive advantage if the unexpected happens.

eg

Shell plans ahead

Shell is an advocate of scenario planning and is reported to have been well prepared at the outbreak of the Gulf war, as it had a plan ready which was based on the scenario of terrorists shutting down a large percentage of available oil wells. If rationing and supply shortages had become an issue, Shell would have had a significant advantage over competitors who were addressing the situation with a blank sheet of paper. Public sector organizations are also expert scenario planners although much of their very detailed work is related to disaster scenarios.

Using the environmental audit

As you can see, monitoring the environment needs to be a constant activity. But lists of opportunities and threats, no matter how well observed, are a waste unless they are used to inform management thinking.

Marketers have to review the environmental information to identify its implications for business activity – summarized as which products should be offered to which markets. Threats restrict the current activities and opportunities available, whilst the opportunities represent the alternative strategies open to grow the business and which will provide the basis for any planned development. The four strategic alternatives can be summarized using the Ansoff Matrix – see Fig. 5.4.

The Ansoff Matrix is often used as a simple four box matrix, but it should really be viewed as a set of two continuums, one indicating the relative newness of products and the other the relative newness of markets. The 'newer' the product the greater the likely investment needed in R&D and the higher the risk associated with new product failure. The newer the market the greater the requirement for market research, investment in new channel development and awareness building.

Fig 5.4 The Ansoff Matrix

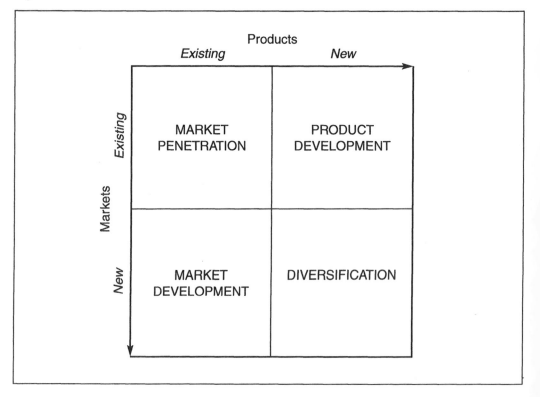

- Use the Ansoff Matrix as a framework for brainstorming the alternatives open to you.
- Ask what the opportunities are for diversification or development to prompt creative review and evaluation of the options.
- Do not get confused if environmental issues seem to be both opportunities and threats – they often are. Management can take steps to turn threats into opportunities, which is why advance warning is vital to planners. For example, economic recession may threaten sales and customer spending but opens up the opportunity for you to gain market share by launching a new 'value for money' range of products.

Use the analysis of your business and your external environment as a basis for helping you to forecast likely sales, profits or activity if you were to take the strategic option of doing nothing, i.e. continuing next year as you have done this – the same products targeted and the same markets.

The bottom line

The trend line in Fig. 5.5 is the base from which the strategic planner must work. It is a useful means of communicating your forecast of the likely business fortunes with no action taken to influence the outcome. I call it the 'do nothing' line. Your market may be in growth or more significant decline, but that is the reality of the situation you must address. Use the grid in Fig. 5.6 to chart out a forecast for your business.

Fig 5.5 The bottom line

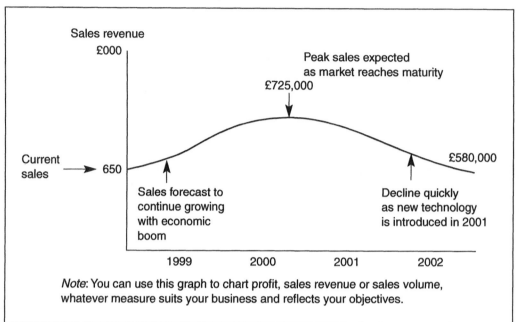

Sales revenue
£000

Peak sales expected
as market reaches maturity
£725,000

Current
sales → 650

£580,000

Sales forecast to
continue growing
with economic
boom

Decline quickly
as new technology
is introduced in 2001

1999   2000   2001   2002

Note: You can use this graph to chart profit, sales revenue or sales volume,
whatever measure suits your business and reflects your objectives.

Forecasting business fortunes

There are a number of factors which should influence
demand and your forecast:

- the stage of the product life cycle
- the economic forecasts – the trade cycle
- changes in competitor activity
- changes in customer preference or behaviour.

Create your own checklists of relevant environmental indicators
as a basis for your future environmental auditing. Try to be as
precise as possible, e.g. new house building statistics and
marriage rates may be useful indicators for furniture
manufacturers. Use the grids on pages 128–9 as a framework.

Fig 5.6 Business forecast grid

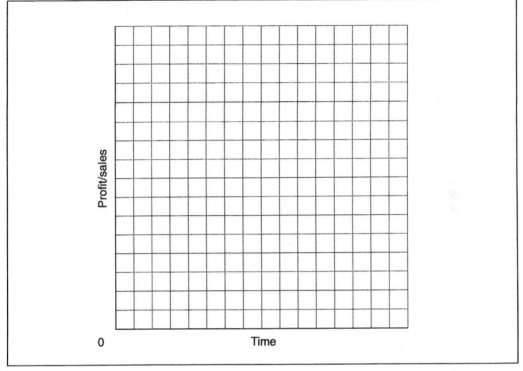

Fig 5.7a Environmental audit

The external environment for _____	
Opportunities	**Threats**

Political and legal

Opportunities	Threats
•	•
•	•
•	•
•	•
•	•
•	•
•	•
•	•
•	•
•	•
•	•

Economic and demographic

Opportunities	Threats
•	•
•	•
•	•
•	•
•	•
•	•
•	•
•	•
•	•
•	•

Fig 5.7b Environmental audit

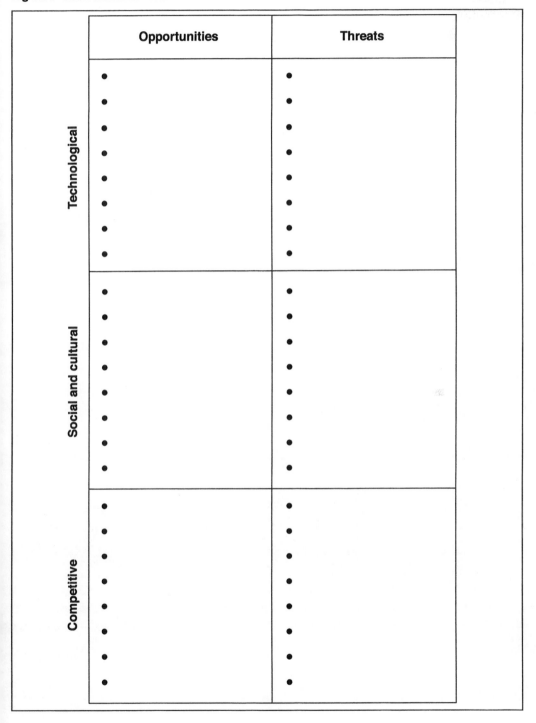

CHAPTER 6

Where are we going?

Raising the corporate umbrella

The corporate mission and vision

Corporate or business objectives

Completing the planning gap

Filling the planning gap

Communicating the strategy

Raising the corporate umbrella

The function of the business plan is to provide a focus for the activities of the organization. By setting a clear goal, communicating a vision and mission for the business, and establishing a strategy to achieve it everyone involved in the plan's implementation can pull together. This integration of effort creates the synergy of value-added outputs (2+2=5) – the basis for the planner to get more from less.

In this chapter we will consider:

- the planning significance and role of the vision and mission
- the characteristics of good corporate objectives and the planning gap
- using a multi-factor matrix to evaluate alternative strategies
- the contribution of marketing to the evalution process
- communicating the corporate strategy.

The corporate mission and vision

The very words 'mission' and 'vision' may have made you groan. Those who have suffered agonizing meetings, debating every word in a mission statement understandably quake at the prospect of revisiting the process. For those whose organization does not boast a mission the creation of one possibly seems like a theoretical exercise and a complete waste of time.

In fact both mission and vision, if used correctly, represent very important building blocks for the planning process. If you go back to the analogy of business as a game the mission statement lays out the parameters of the pitch on which we are playing. We already had to answer the question, 'what business are we in?' to create our market map. Once a mission is established, managers have clear limits indicating which areas of activity they should address, and this is the first step in consolidating the focus of the organization's activities.

- The mission statement has been somewhat hijacked from this central planning function. It has been adopted as a public relations statement targeted at all of the organization's stakeholders – featured prominently in annual reports and at shareholders' meetings. It is because of this public spotlight that managers debate long and hard about every word and comma, adding messages for every audience and striving hard to give offence to no one.
- The result is often long-winded and complex; it conveys little of the uniqueness of the organization, its culture or area of activity. The standard 'being nice to staff, children and trees', which seems to creep into many missions, makes it difficult for employees to recognize their own companies from these publicized statements.
- If staff feel like this, and if managers are paying lip service to an idealized and unrealistic mission, the attitude to the whole planning process is likely to be cynical and unproductive.

The mission of the business should lay down clearly the answer to the question, 'what business are we in or should we be in?' The answer to this question should be customer, not product, oriented. Consider these two possible answers:

- we are in the business of manufacturing small cars
- our business provides travellers in space-sensitive environments with comfortable, compact and cost-effective personal transportation.

This second version indicates much more about the business and its targeted user groups. From this, drivers in Japan would be a more natural target than those in Australia, and city dwellers rather than rural residents. A manager working for this firm would know that a strategy to introduce a large, petrol-hungry, stretched-body model would not be consistent with the mission. An opportunity to introduce a range of small motorized bicycles would be worth consideration – it leaves the corporate positioning intact.

- Remember you can only plan effectively at strategic business unit level – even a large college may need to establish a number of SBUs to reflect the diversity of its activities. A single umbrella mission for the whole organization would have little value or role in the strategic planning of activities in a complex operation.
- Do not make the mistake of thinking that mission statements are written in tablets of stone. They can be challenged and changed, but this should not be done too regularly because for planners it is the equivalent of moving the goalposts!

Mission statement checklist

A useful mission statement should:

- identify customer benefits
- answer the question of what business you are in
- indicate any limitations to the sphere of activity – for example, operating in the North American market or in consumer services
- make benefits to shareholders implicit – to say you are in business to make a profit is not a mission, but many organizations add reference to such stakeholder benefits
- make clear any cultural or organizational values which are central to the business and must be adhered to by it planners. The Body Shop's commitment to the environment would be appropriately included.

The vision

The vision is more of a long-term goal. It is important that the managing director has a vision of the business in 10 years and is able to share this with others. It provides the long-distance focus for strategy and can be the goal others aspire to achieve. The vision probably will not be quantified, but it may incorporate sentiments of excellence. You may, for example, want to be number one in leading-edge virtual reality technology for the consumer market or a team manager may have the vision of winning the Superbowl and the charity of eradicating malnutrition in Somalia. These longer-term targets are important to motivation and give all stakeholders a sense of purpose which they can understand and share.

The vision, then, establishes the horizon for the planning activity, and the mission lays down the parameters of the activities which will be undertaken to achieve the mission.

A note on competitive positioning

The vision and mission go some way to helping establish an overall corporate positioning and set of values against which the corporate brand will be built or reinforced. The social and ethical positioning of the Co-operative Bank in the UK or the convenience and accessibility which were the founding principles behind Coca-Cola are examples of this.

Corporate or business objectives

These are the quantified targets which a plan, usually set for one, three or five years, will seek to deliver.

!!!

- Do not think that a general desire to increase sales will suffice as an objective. To be of any value an objective must be specific, so the activity can be controlled. It must therefore be quantified.
- Similarly, do not set objectives which you expect to be exceeded – the plan is intended to co-ordinate resources. If you sell more than planned you will find you are short of supply, unless the variation has been fed back to operational staff in time for them to modify output.
- Objectives set too high will be perceived as unrealistic and are more likely to demotivate than to inspire staff to try harder.

Objectives checklist

To be of use any plan must have an objective which is:

- **Specific**
- **Measurable**
- **Achievable**
- **Relevant** – has meaning to those expected to deliver it
- **Timed.**

Corporate objectives

The overall objectives of the business plan will normally be expressed in benefits to the stakeholders. This after all is the purpose of the business activity, whether it be to generate profits in the private sector, improve health or education levels in the community, or generate funds for a charity. To ensure that objectives are achievable they need to be tested against key environmental and situational considerations.

Ambitious objectives will be appropriate in the following situations:

- in growth markets
- when competition is limited
- when growth is through acquisition
- in buoyant economic conditions
- when resources are available for expansion.

Conservative objectives will be more appropriate:

- in mature markets
- when facing increasing competition
- when growth is evolutionary
- in depressed economic conditions
- when resources are limited.

Check out your own business plan. What objectives have been set and do they satisfy the SMART criteria?

Completing the planning gap

The first step when identifying the planning gap was the trend line laid down following the corporate audit (see chapter 5, page 126). By setting your corporate objective against this you can clearly calculate the size of the planning challenge being faced – see Fig. 6.1 below.

This process is a good test of an objective's achievability. Managers can clearly see the extent of the gap between current and targeted outcomes – the extent of performance improvement required will be obvious and will soon be commented upon. If it is seen as unjustifiably ambitious, now is the time it can be reviewed.

Fig 6.1 Establishing the planning gap

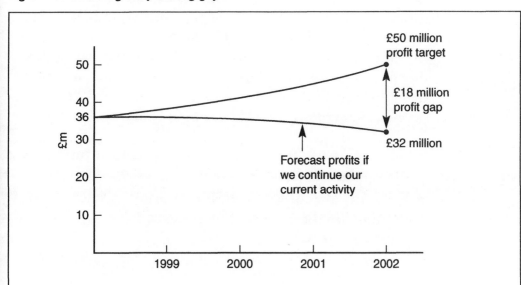

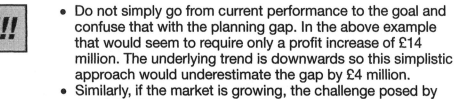

- Do not simply go from current performance to the goal and confuse that with the planning gap. In the above example that would seem to require only a profit increase of £14 million. The underlying trend is downwards so this simplistic approach would underestimate the gap by £4 million.
- Similarly, if the market is growing, the challenge posed by the objectives may be insignificant when considered against the upward trend.

Do not confuse the picture unnecessarily. Round numbers up or down, and deal as at today's prices. If you start trying to correct for inflation in five years' time you will be lost and the basic message of the planning gap will become meaningless. Your fundamental strategy will be the same, and based on the assumption that your price level keeps pace with inflation, your objective will be achieved anyway.

Use the grid in Fig. 6.2 to produce a planning gap for your business over the next three years – work in profit or revenue.

Ideally the private sector business plan should be set against profit because it is easy to raise revenue without necessarily increasing profits. For example, firm A generates £1,000,000 revenue and has a gross profit margin of 20 per cent, generating a gross profit of £200,000. The senior management team want to grow the business and develop a number of strategies to fill a planning gap of another million pounds of revenue:

- they target larger corporate clients who are attracted by a discount to them of 5 per cent
- they hire an additional sales person and increase the promotional budget – a cost increase equal to 2 per cent of targeted revenue

Fig 6.2 Planning gap grid

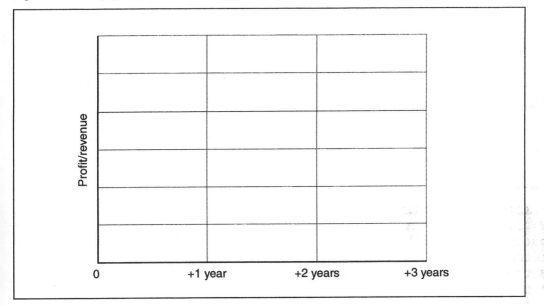

- the products typically ordered by bigger clients generated average gross profits of less than the 20 per cent achieved before – gross margins to these new clients are only 17 per cent.

The first £1 million revenue generated earned £200,000 profit. The second million generated only £100,000 profit:

17%	margin on products
–2%	increase in promotional costs
–5%	price discount
10%	margin

Profits in total have increased but it is easy to see how you can end up doing more for less. Had the objective been set to increase profits from £200,000 to £400,000 the selected strategies may have been different.

Checklist for the financial impact of marketing strategies

Marketing planners should keep on reminding themselves that three decisions they make can directly influence profitability:

- changing the mix of customers
- changing the mix of products
- changing the marketing mix.

Filling the planning gap

Now you know what you are trying to achieve, where you are starting from and the alternative strategies available to you.

In practice most organizations will employ a combination of strategies implemented over time to fill the planning gap. There is a limit to the options open to you if you are looking at a short-term objective. In one or two years you can probably do little to introduce new products and so may need to rely on market penetration and market development strategies. Longer-term plans can consider product development and diversification strategies. The strategic options need to be evaluated and selected to fill the planning gap.

Selecting strategies

The opportunities identified now need evaluation to allow you to select those which best match the competitive competences that the business can offer. Forecasts of potential earnings must be made so that the likely contribution of each strategy to the overall objective can be quantified.

Do not make the mistake of treating all your identified opportunities as equally valuable and therefore make them equal substitutes for one another. Launching a new product with a revenue potential of £10 million will take as much management time as one with a potential 10 times as great.

A number of evaluation methods exist. You might find completing a SWOT analysis for each identified alternative reveals quite a lot about their suitability for the business; however, this is a fairly crude approach.

Using the multi-factor matrix

A particularly useful technique is the multi-factor matrix, which we have already examined in depth in chapter 4. The process is exactly the same as that used for portfolio analysis:

- management must identify and weight the criteria by which they would judge an opportunity to be attractive
- marketing staff undertake research with the potential customers to identify and weight criteria by which they would make purchase decisions
- each strategy or opportunity is scored against both sets of criteria to establish a score for opportunity attractiveness and likely competitive advantage
- feasibility studies or cost benefit analysis are undertaken to forecast likely sales revenue or profit from each opportunity
- this information is plotted on the matrix – see Fig. 6.3.

In this way, selected strategies are not only certain to be attractive to the business, but are also customer-oriented, i.e. the potential for competitive success has been taken into account.

Fig 6.3 Comparing strategies

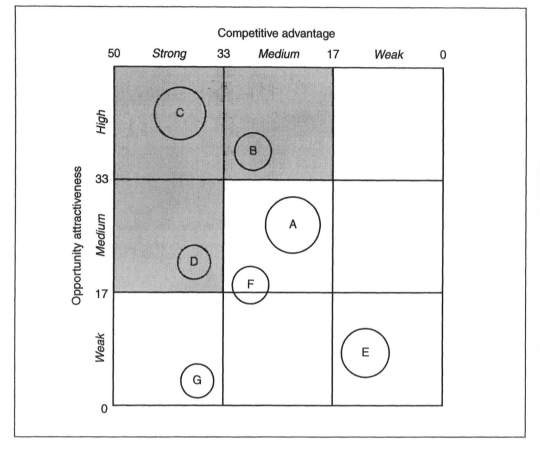

- If your objectives are short term, make sure you weight the speed of return highly in your management criteria.
- If your available investment resources are limited, then this requires emphasis.
- Each opportunity can be placed on the grid. The size of the circles indicates revenue forecasts. Here B, C and D look the most attractive.

Fig 6.4 Strategies for closing the planning gap

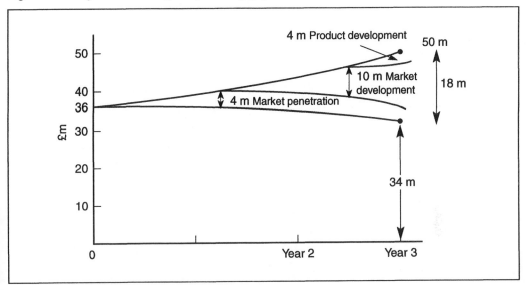

Strategic sub-objectives can now be identified:

- to have gained an additional £4 million profit through market penetration by end of year 1
- to have generated an additional £10 million profit from newly developed markets by year 3
- to launch a new product in year 3 which contributes £4 million to total profits by year 5.

Do not concentrate all your efforts on filling the gap and neglect the core business. A fourth objective is implicit in this scenario – to retain profits from the core customer base equal to £34 million by the end of year 5.

- In practice you can only ascribe values to each strategy after the strategic options have been selected and their feasible contribution calculated, but this overview demonstrates the idea behind the process.
- For each strategic sub-objective selected you will need to develop a detailed marketing plan for implementation. So if you select 10 strategies to fill a gap you need 11 plans, including the one for customer retention.

Communicating the strategy

Once the management team has selected strategies, it has established the heart of the business plan. Its tactics – the detail of the plan's implementation – will be provided by the functional teams; marketing, finance and operations. Their efforts will be harmonized because they are all clearly focused to achieve the same objectives via the same strategies. This will be effective as long as strategy is clearly communicated – for example, to generate profits of £4 million by launching our current range to business customers in the Italian market.

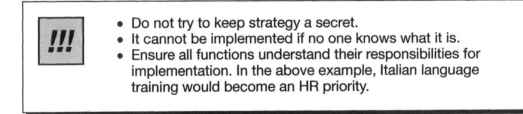

- Do not try to keep strategy a secret.
- It cannot be implemented if no one knows what it is.
- Ensure all functions understand their responsibilities for implementation. In the above example, Italian language training would become an HR priority.

Selling strategy

Teams who have been involved in the planning process up to this point are likely to be more committed to the agreed strategy. But it will still need presenting and promoting to staff if they are to be motivated by it. Staff support is an important ingredient for success and cannot simply be assumed. That requires a coherent internal marketing strategy – see chapter 10.

- Even if your business is smaller and planning relatively straightforward, involving few staff, this corporate umbrella needs to be raised so that you can plan and co-ordinate your efforts and resources constructively.
- The process described in this chapter can be completed on the back of an envelope, but a clear objective and strategy must be established. Remember if you don't know or care where you are going, any route will get you there. If you do care, that destination must be clearly established and an agreed route laid out for all to follow.

CHAPTER 7

Implementing corporate strategy

Developing the market strategy

Components of a marketing plan

The marketing background

Integrating the marketing mix

Developing the market strategy

Up until this point in the process the marketing team has been adding to or undertaking work related to the development of the business plan. For the organization to become customer oriented this marketing input and involvement with corporate strategy is vital.

From this stage onwards the marketer is concerned with his or her contribution to the successful implementation of that agreed business strategy. In common with the other functional areas, marketing now needs to develop its own plan for each strand of strategy detailed at the corporate level.

Each strategy requires a separate set of operational plans to implement it – see Fig. 7.1. In this book we are concentrating only on the marketing plan, but other functional plans require developing and co-ordinating to ensure an integrated marketing mix is established for each strategy.

Fig 7.1 Operational plans for business strategy

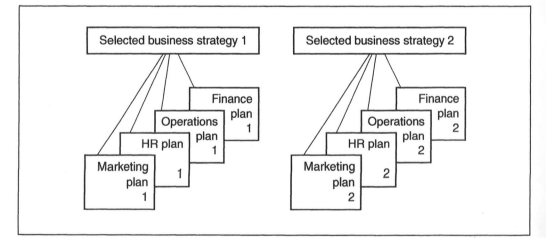

In this chapter we will be examining the transition from corporate strategy to marketing strategy, including:

- overviewing the components of an operational marketing plan
- the establishment of relevant marketing objectives and a marketing planning gap
- the elements of marketing strategy:
  - segmentation: why? how?
  - positioning
  - targeting.

Components of a marketing plan

Over the following chapters we will be working through the steps and elements which lead to the creation of a marketing plan. Before beginning that process it will perhaps be helpful to overview the output of that activity – the marketing plan and its components. In Fig. 7.2 you can see the skeleton of the plan on the right and a summary of the relevant planning process on the left.

The marketing background

Any plan needs to be prepared so that it stands alone, can be read by someone outside the business or in years to come, and has a clear rationale. It is not possible to judge the quality of a marketing plan without knowledge of the starting point (audit) and the corporate scenario against which it has been produced.

Be specific

The planning process works best if you start off with the big picture (the business plan), with a sense of the scale and shape of things, and then gradually as you work down the planning

Fig 7.2 Marketing plan skeleton

Process ⟶	Plan
Audits – will already have been completed to inform the situational analysis; but may be refined to relate specifically to this product/market area.	**Background** – including a review of limiting factors and critical success factors drawn from the audit, and an outline of the corporate strategy and objectives this plan intends to deliver.
Objectives – derived directly from the corporate direction but need careful calculation to identify what revenue is needed to generate the profits targeted.	**Objectives** – the corporate (profit based) objectives will be made relevant by conversion to marketing objectives expressed in terms of: • customers • revenue • market share • occupancy/utilization.
Strategy development – the hard part of the process: • methods of market segmentation are identified and evaluated • a market segmentation approach is selected and segments within it checked for feasibility – requiring further research into customer needs and profiles in that segment • an appropriate positioning is agreed upon • decisions arrived at which must be repeated if targeting more than one market segment.	**Strategy** – answers the question of how these objectives will be achieved. The plan should include a profile of the selected market segments. It should confirm the established market positioning and state the approach if more than one segment is targeted.

Fig 7.2 Continued

Tactics – depending on the size of the organization, named individuals may now be allocated responsibility for tactical planning. This is particularly likely in the area of promotion. Decisions within other functional areas must be co-ordinated as they impact on the Ps of the marketing mix. The planning process must be repeated for each tactical activity: • where are we now? • where are we going? • how do we get there? • action plan • controls.	**Tactics** – as with the business plan, marketing strategy serves to co-ordinate the action plans at the next level of implementation. Detailed objectives and actions for each element of the marketing mix will be included in tactics.
Controls – who does what, when and for how much represent the bridge from planning to action, requiring considerable planning effort.	**Controls** – details of feedback mechanisms, the budget and timetable conclude the formal plan.

hierarchy add more detail. You may therefore need to take a little time to refine your background analysis to reflect the specifics of this segment of the business. For instance, whilst the market's awareness of your brand generally might run at 60 per cent in this segment of the market, it may actually be 80 per cent. Buyer behaviour may have its peculiarities and there may be some specific issues related to distribution or promotion which would be worth highlighting.

- Do not be tempted to turn this part of your plan into a history of the business. It should be short and to the point but carry as many of the critical factors as possible.
- Any supporting evidence and information which you feel needs to be included can be added as appendices.
- Planning is focused on the future so information about the past and present provides reference points but does little to move the business forward.

Translating corporate-marketing objectives

At the end of chapter 6 we identified how revenue and profits do not necessarily increase at the same rate. The marketer can seldom just assume that doubling sales will double profits; he or she must also consider the impact of the strategies being proposed.

- Note that throughout the planning activity there needs to be a considerable amount of negotiation – top down and bottom up. This is the planning process and must be completed before plans can be written up.
- In the planning process a working objective will be established, but this may later need reviewing in light of further research and assessment once a strategy has been selected.
- In the completed plans the specific objectives will be decisive and feature early in the documents.

The planning gap model is again very useful here because it helps you to visualize what is going on. By including not only a line for revenue but also the profit margin, managers can be sure they consider the financial implications of their strategy.

In Fig. 7.3 you can see how at the beginning of the planning process the business was generating £10,000 profit on a turnover of £50,000 from this product (a 20 per cent margin).

Fig 7.3 Market strategies

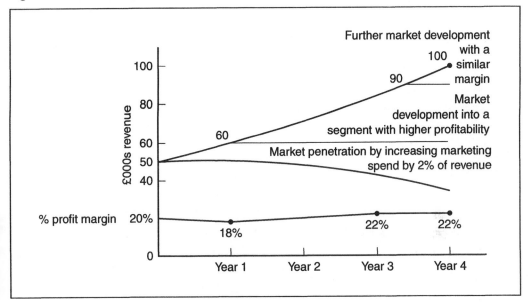

The short-term strategy of market penetration is planned to generate £10,000 additional sales revenue, but this is to be achieved by an increase in marketing effort. This might mean more distribution, promotion or price incentives, but it is planned to spend an additional 2 per cent of revenue on marketing (2 per cent of £60,000 = £1,200 increase in marketing budget).

In the longer term, strategies of market development are expected to have generated an increase in margin of 22 per cent, so by year 4, double the turnover has more than doubled profits – £22,000 on £100,000 sales.

An objective cascade

Marketing objectives are not created from thin air. They are calculated from the business objective already established to do this calculation. You will need to make an assumption or forecast about gross profit margins or price levels. These should have been informed by your earlier analysis. For example, if Porter's five forces analysis indicated margins tightening you would build in that assumption here.

Don't worry about your forecasts proving inaccurate. One of the first controls you will establish will be to monitor the margin or average price, etc.

If a strategy is forecast to contribute £100,000 profit to the overal planning gap and, assuming a 10 per cent gross profit margin, the marketing objective is to generate £1 million revenue.

This objective could be expressed as a volume objective. If you assume the average selling price is £100, the 10,000 units need to be sold and if the total market was to equal 100,000 units, this means achieving an extra 10 per cent market share.

Revenue, market share and volume are *not* different objectives. They are the same objective expressed differently. Every plan needs a *single* clear objective.

Take care using market share as an objective. Market share is difficult to measure, it depends on your definition of the market and it is unlikely to be static. It can, however, be a useful reality check. An objective which requires you to increase your share of a mature market by 10 per cent may be unrealistic, whereas a 1 per cent target may be quite feasible.

Relevant objectives

The intention is to create objectives that have meaning to those trying to achieve them. Sales revenue may be adequate, but wherever possible it is better to convert these into customer numbers because staff can usually more easily relate to the implications of this growth target on the day-to-day running of the business.

---

eg

Calculating conference clients

Consider the case of a conference hotel, currently operating at 60 per cent occupancy. It has 100 rooms and a 24-hour delegate rate of £200. The board is asking for profits to be increased by £0.5 million. The marketing director has translated this into a marketing objective of 70 per cent occupancy (10 more rooms per night x £200 x 365 nights a year = £730,000 revenue). Margins are around 65 per cent because only marginal costs will be incurred by raising occupancy.

The marketing team can see its objectives in terms of total room sales revenue and occupancy, but these may still not be the most relevant measures for the staff.

Assuming the average booking was a three-night stay for 30 people, the marketer can now give the team a customer-based objective:

$$\text{Objective: } \frac{3{,}650 \text{ more room nights}}{3 \times 30 \text{ room nights average booking}}$$

$$\frac{3{,}650}{90} = \text{approx. 40 additional conference bookings.}$$

Strategies to achieve this more relevant expression of the extra performance needed can now be determined and effort targeted to fill seasonality gaps or to increase repeat purchases from past users. Similarly, the operational and staffing requirements are also more obvious and can help focus other functional plans.

Do not feel constrained by the objective-setting process. As long as your intentions are relevant, perceived to be achievable and quantified over time, you will find they help to focus your business energies.

Whilst the business plan may cover a relatively long time-frame, the planning horizon for the marketing plan is more normally medium term – often one year but more effectively three years, possibly up to five years. This is because the market conditions change so rapidly that longer time-scales are of relatively little use.

Take time to work through from your business objectives to marketing ones. Review the impact of different strategies and then convert your objectives to customer targets where possible.

Determining marketing strategy

The heart of any plan is the strategy. It is so easy for people in any activity to agree on an objective but then set about achieving it in different ways. The resulting lack of co-ordination inevitably means, at best, wasted resources, at worst, a lack of progress as people on the same side work against each other.

Consider your own organization. If it is filled with well-intentioned staff, working hard and achieving little, then you can be fairly sure that the cause is a lack of strategy – either in the business or marketing plans.

Marketing plans surprisingly frequently have a strategic black hole. They start with the objectives but then jump to the marketing tactics. But the strategy is critical. It is the strategy which stops business trying to be all things to all people.

No organization can be 'best' at everything, nor can they be all things to all people. The concept of market segmentation introduces the notion of selectivity – concentrating resources on the needs of a small part of the total market. In this way the specific needs of that group can be satisfied, whilst direct head-to-head competition becomes less likely as market players differentiate their offerings to appeal to different segments.

The philosophy of marketing is based on this concentration of efforts and specialization. When there is competition it is better to be the preferred supplier to some groups of customers than to try to compete for the whole market. Marketing strategy answers the questions:

- Which group(s) of customers?
- Why should they prefer us?

Market segmentation

Because of this key role it is perhaps not surprising that the activity of market segmentation is critical to the effectiveness of the marketing plan. It is a process that must be undertaken with thought, creativity and skill.

It is not enough simply to find a descriptive way to break a market up. To have any value those within the segment must have something in common, something which allows marketers to serve their needs specifically and more effectively than the competitors. If age, sex, company size or a customer's location significantly influence buyer behaviour, then these will be useful dimensions for segmentation. If not, you need to find new bases for your segmentation.

Segmenting markets

There are few limits as to how you can segment a market, and new creative approaches can open up new market opportunities. Techniques for business to business markets are somewhat different but still reflect the same principles as consumer markets. Ask yourself how the market is segmented in your industry. Are there different approaches which might be used?

Consumer markets

Geo-demographic variables are perhaps most commonly associated with segmentation. Age, sex, ethnic background and geographic location represent variables that are easy to identify and that in some markets do influence behaviour.

A retailer may choose to serve the women's market with clothes selected for 30–50-year-olds. A range of saris would attract the local Indian population, whilst a good selection of business suits would satisfy the needs of locally based working women. Styles and quality would influence the socio-economic profile of the targeted shoppers. Cocktail and evening dresses would attract higher-income social groups.

Improved database management has dramatically changed an organization's ability to use these sorts of profiles to target customers. Traditionally in the UK socio-economic groupings were very much linked with class. The social groups indicate preferences, tastes and aspirations which go on to influence what each group would buy and how much it could afford to spend. The key groups are:

A – upper social classes, such as industry leaders, MPs, etc.
B – professional classes
C1 – white-collar workers, office staff
C2 – skilled blue-collar workers, trade and craft people
D – unskilled blue-collar workers, factory staff and labourers
E – disadvantaged social groups – such as pensioners, students and the unemployed.

These groupings are still often referred to as a sort of marketing shorthand, but better profiling systems are now available.

For example, ACORN analysis uses UK housing types as a means of breaking the population into over 40 categories. Information is linked to the postcodes and census information, so organizations can now identify the names and addresses of people living in flats or large, detached properties within a specified geographic area. Whilst expensive to acquire, such lists improve the effectiveness of your marketing activity considerably.

Segmenting by product use
People often buy the same generic product, but to satisfy different needs. A person may buy a bicycle for racing, fitness, social or work motives. Training shoes may be brought as a fashion accessory, for amateur or profesional sport, or as comfortable, casual footwear. These different motives for purchase are an extremely relevant approach to market segmentation. Whatever the customers' geodemographic or socio-economic profile, their buying needs and priorities are likely to be similar.

Can your market be segmented according to product use or customer behaviour? Would this impact on the way in which you serviced the market?

You are also likely to have some customers who are more regular or loyal clients, and who spend more with you than others. Which of these segments is the most attractive/profitable to you? You might have identified them during your initial audit activities.

Analysis of your existing customer base may allow you to classify customers as:

- light users – occasional clients
- medium users – regular clients
- heavy users – loyal clients.

It is very expensive to attract new users, and the chances are they will at first become light users, requiring time and effort from you to convert them to more regular or heavy users. Your heavy users are already loyal to you and you may already be earning as much as you can from them. The greatest potential is often from increasing sales to light and medium users, who are already aware of you and identifiable for targeted promotional efforts by you.

Further analysis of these segments of your customer base may reveal characteristics that help you to profile potential future heavy users. This will provide you with information to segment further medium and light users and target your marketing effort even more precisely – effective strategies for market penetration.

Psychographic and lifestyle segmentation
As our study of customer behaviour has developed, so it has been possible to identify bases for segmentation related to motivations, aspirations and attitudes. We know people's behaviour is influenced by the stage of the family life cycle they are at. For example, a single person will have different holiday needs to a couple with young children. Segments like 'Dinkies' and 'Empty Nesters' have entered the vocabulary of managers. 'Dinkies' are dual-income families with no kids, whereas 'Empty Nesters' are couples with a grown family who have left home. 'Yuppies' were the upwardly mobile young professionals who brought us the Filofax and mobile phones, and who represented a major boost for the sales of Porsche cars in the mid-1980s.

You can segment a market by shades of green, reflecting people's views on the environment, or by the element of risk they like in their lives. A variety of techniques and profiles have been generated that you can adapt or use.

★

- Remember that the segment needs to reflect characteristics that are relevant to buying behaviour.
- A segment needs to be big enough to satisfy your objectives – a segment of 100 is of limited value if you are targeting sales of 10,000. Similarly 10,000 is too large if you are looking for 100 – it would represent a considerable waste of marketing effort. If your analysis shows you have a conversion rate of 1:10, you would need to target only 1,000 prospects to generate the desired 100 additional sales.

Business to business segments

Those serving industrial clients need to segment their market in a similar way. Their task is often easier because numbers involved are usually smaller and easily identified. A closer working relationship means characteristics and buying behaviour may be known in more detail.

There are a number of common starting points for business to business segmentation:

- company size
  - by employees
  - by turnover
- geographic coverage
  - local/regional/national/international catchment
  - location
- industry/sector
- product use
  - volume of use
  - purpose of use
- buying behaviour
  - level of decision-making
  - loyalty demonstrated
  - contract approach, e.g. by tender
  - price sensitivity
  - availability and support needs.

Even business to business markets must take care not simply to segment the market by industry or company size because it is easy to do so. Not enough attention is being paid to buying behaviour and needs across commercial segments and companies like Dell Computers, which has established direct sell to experienced buyers and has found considerable competitive advantage through effective segmentation.

Whatever your business, its size or sector, you will find the process of market segmentation a valuable one. The key to getting more from less marketing resources is the focus imposed by segmentation. The tighter your segmentation analysis and the more sophisticated your approach the more effective your efforts will be.

- Remember there are two dimensions to selecting the right segment.
- It is not enough simply to choose the one that looks the most profitable; you need to be able to offer those customers real benefits, and you must be able to sustain a competitive advantage in that segment.

Choosing and evaluating segments

Again, strategic decisions must be made by the planner and once again the multi-factor matrix is a flexible framework for helping the marketing team to compare the attractiveness of alternative segments that could be targeted. It allows the rating of both segment attractiveness and likely customer attractiveness (i.e. competitive advantage) – see Fig. 7.4. The steps are the same, as were detailed for evaluating corporate strategy (see chapter 6).

Fig 7.4 Comparing the attractiveness of segments

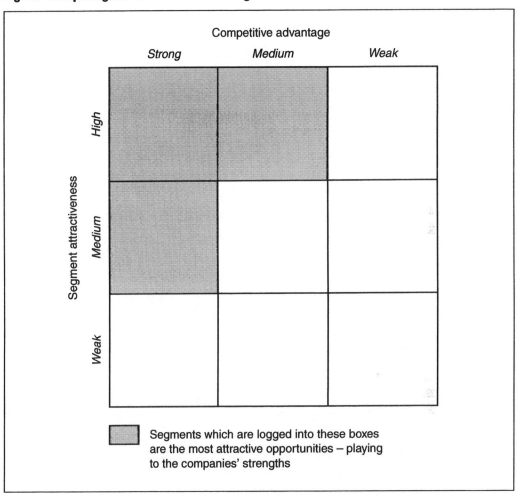

Management's criteria, however, may differ, reflecting, for example, concerns over the:

- size of segment
- forecast growth
- price sensitivity of segment
- degree of competition for the segment
- costs of accessing the segment
- forecast risk.

- Once a segment has been selected it is worth checking that it meets the required characteristics of a 'good segment' from the checklist below.
- Being able to define a customer group is one thing, but it is only of value if you can then make contact with those defined customers.

A segmentation checklist

To be of use a market segment must be:

- *substantial* – big enough to make the marketing effort cost-effective
- *unique* – so it can be distinguished from other market segments
- *appropriate* – in that it fits with the organization's objectives and resources
- *accessible* – so it can be identified and reached by the marketing activities of the team.

In addition, it is helpful if a segment is stable and measurable as this helps with forecasting and control.

Market positioning of a segment

Once a segment has been identified and selected, an appropriate market positioning can be developed. To do this, first review the key variables which influence this segment's purchase decisions and use these as the basis of your positioning maps to communicate the various dimensions of your offering, but be certain all positions are internally consistent with one another – see Fig. 7.5.

The variables of the marketing mix can be used as the axes for your positioning maps – image factors like modern or traditional, and product factors like basic functional to deluxe with added features are equally valid.

Fig 7.5 Positioning maps

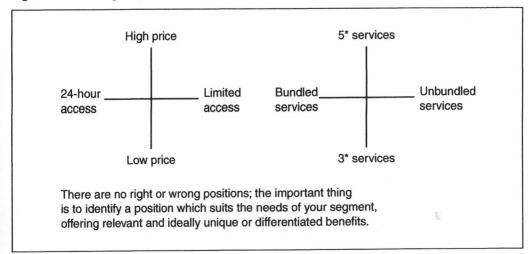

High price

24-hour access — Limited access

Low price

5* services

Bundled services — Unbundled services

3* services

There are no right or wrong positions; the important thing
is to identify a position which suits the needs of your segment,
offering relevant and ideally unique or differentiated benefits.

Integrating the marketing mix

It is the positioning map which will ensure that all your
marketing mix decisions are co-ordinated or integrated. The
marketing manager is like the conductor of an orchestra. All
the elements of the marketing mix, like musical instruments,
can be brought in. Some may feature more strongly but if
the result is to be harmonious then all the elements must be
playing the same tune. The positioning map is the marketer's sheet music.

- Remember that positioning maps are a useful way of
  comparing your product with that of the competitor.
- Avoiding competitive confrontation requires you to focus on
  a different segment of the market (see chapter 3) serving a
  specific group of customers to whom you can become a
  preferred supplier.

> Do not develop a positioning without reference to the customers in your segment. The benefits a position offers can only be judged by the extent to which it satisfies customer needs.

Targeting

One segment of the market may not be sufficient to fill the marketing planning gap, or it may not be wise to depend on just one segment. If you are targeting more than one segment you will need to decide on what approach you will adopt with each. You may retain a consistent approach, targeted at a number of segments, or choose to differentiate your activities to meet the needs of each segment.

The approach in Fig. 7.6 uses a consistency of marketing activity to ensure control and lower marketing costs because of marketing economies of scale.

By tailoring each offering to each segment (see Fig. 7.7), the product should more closely satisfy customer needs in each segment and so increase the revenue earned from each – making the higher costs justified.

Fig 7.6 Undifferentiated marketing

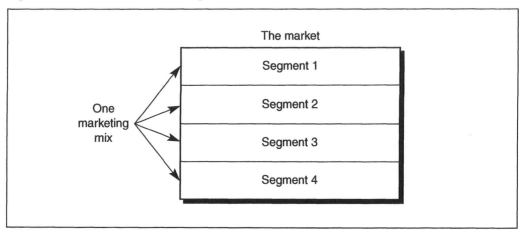

Fig 7.7 Differentiated marketing

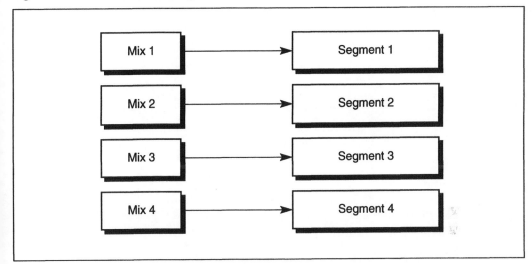

If you decide on a differentiated strategy then each segment will require its own positioning and tactical plan.

The three elements of segmentation, positioning and targeting make up marketing strategy. Decisions made at this stage are the essential starting points for the tactical plans and must be communicated clearly to those expected to produce the details for implementation. It is very important to recognize that other functional areas can also have a significant impact on the various elements of the mix. Use Fig. 7.8 to work out your proposed positioning.

Take time to examine the positioning and potential positioning for your product or service. Consider plotting your product on more than one map using more than one set of variables. Specify the profile of each segment of the market you are targeting and decide whether or not to differentiate your marketing approach to them.

Fig 7.8 A proposed postioning for...

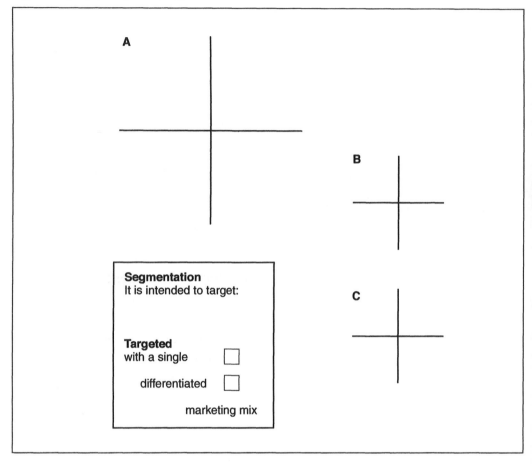

CHAPTER 8

Planning for the 7Ps

The tactics of the marketing mix

Why do customers buy?

Price

Promotion

Place

The extended service mix

People

Physical evidence

Processes

Action

The tactics of the marketing mix

The details of the marketing plan are included under the heading of tactics. In this section the role of the various elements of the marketing mix are spelt out. Their efforts will be channelled by the positioning and focused on the selected segments of the market.

Depending on the size and nature of the organization this stage in the planning process may be the work of one or many people. The tactics once actioned will be the representation of the company in its marketplace and so will directly impact on the success of the operation. The efficiency of the marketing effort is determined by how well the marketing mix elements can be used to support and reinforce each other – getting more from less marketing resource.

In this chapter we will consider:

- how the marketing mix combines to provide value-for-money offerings
- the way in which customer demand can be influenced by changes in the mix
- the extended mix for services
- the individual elements of the mix:
  - product
  - price
  - promotion (covered in more depth in chapter 9)
  - place
  - physical evidence
  - people
  - processes
- how the mix is characteristically combined in different sectors.

Why do customers buy?

We identified in an earlier chapter that customers buy solutions to their problems. They have needs and require products or services which will satisfy those needs. They are searching for benefits, which is a difficult concept to define because benefits are unique to each individual. A cup of tea will give one person more benefit (economists describe it as utility/usefulness) than his or her neighbour derives from a similar cup. The differences are due to taste, the extent of their thirst and priorities of each tea drinker.

In sector after sector managers and customer contact staff believe their customers buy on price. No one ever buys on price, they choose on $\frac{value}{money}$ – a significantly different proposition. If someone buys a cheaper option he or she is deciding that the more expensive option is the same or offers additional benefits which are of no/low value to him or her. In study after study customers identify clearly that price is less important to them than suppliers would imagine – but customers will only pay more for benefits they value. This does not of course alter the fact that some market segments are more price sensitive than others, but it does provide managers with enough reason to question the importance of price to their users.

Value for money

Every purchase we make is decided by our assessment of value for money – is it worth it? If I do not buy this, how much satisfaction would I get from spending on the alternative on offer?

Faced with limited incomes, individuals and companies have to make choices. They are addressing what economists call the economic problem – limited resources and unlimited needs. Just as we identified when considering the rationale for planning, all purchases are motivated by the need of customers to get more from less. Customers, clients and service users are all motivated to find offerings which give them the most benefit/value for the least outlay.

Marketing is closely related to the study of economics – both are focused on the exchange process, and much of our understanding of marketing has been borrowed from the study of economics. The economists have identified that the individual makes purchase decisions by comparing utility/benefit against price across a range of possible purchases. The selection offering the best value for money is made. Marketers have identified the factors which influence the customer's calculation of value for money and they comprise of the variables of the marketing mix.

6Ps add value

The 6Ps of the extended marketing mix add to perceived value or utility – the seventh is price:

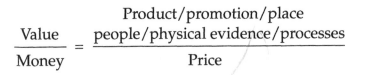

$$\frac{\text{Value}}{\text{Money}} = \frac{\text{Product/promotion/place people/physical evidence/processes}}{\text{Price}}$$

The image of a service, its availability, functionality, the customer care, user-friendly booking system and attractive physical environment would all contribute to the satisfaction you gained from a service experience. How much of any product/service a customer will buy is based on their personal value for money calculation.

Lowering price is one way of increasing demand because the customer is getting the same benefits for less spend – a better deal (see Fig. 8.1).

Fig 8.1 The price/demand relationship

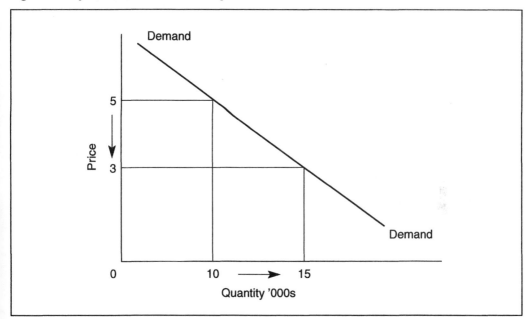

When the price in this example is reduced to 3, sales are expected to increase by 5,000 units. This basic relationship of price to quantity is widely understood and price is frequently used to stimulate sales. If your objective is market share rather than profit maximization, selling on price is likely to help you achieve increased sales.

Try adding value

The alternative approach advocated by marketers is to change demand by adding value. The customer's calculation of benefits for price now encourages more purchases at the original price – see Fig. 8.2.

Adding value by changing the six non-price variables of the mix shifts demand.

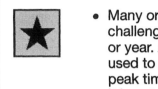

- Many organizations are faced with a different demand challenge – too much demand during peak times of the day or year. At these times the value/money equation can be used to reduce demand – offering only a basic service at peak times, restricting availability and so on.
- It is not always desirable to use higher prices to ration available supply – this approach to demand management will give you an alternative.

Fig 8.2 Changes in price/demand

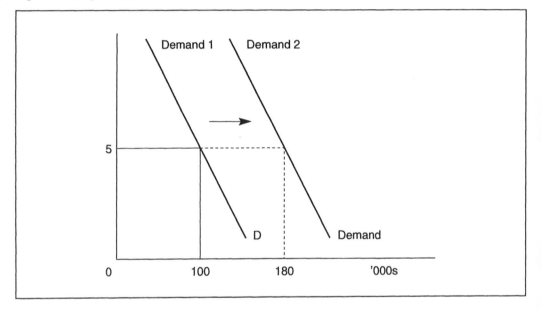

The limited role of price

In practice, price can be shown to be of only limited use in demand management. Not all purchases are sensitive to price. There are some goods you would buy irrespective of price. These goods are termed price inelastic or price insensitive. Tobacco, alcohol, drugs, petrol and basic necessities are all relatively insensitive to price changes.

Understandably, many managers would like their products to be less sensitive to price changes. They could raise prices and pass on cost or tax rises without losing too much business – an attractive proposition. As a result they turn to marketing tactics to give their products the characteristics which make a purchase price inelastic. These price inelastic characteristics are present if the product is:

- a necessity
- without close competitors
- addictive.

Marketers use branding, packaging and advertising to differentiate products from those of close competitors. There may be plenty of detergents, but if you believe Persil washes whiter and value white washing there is no choice.

Even luxury items are positioned as necessities to encourage customers to push them higher up their shopping lists. Finally, promotional activities are used to encourage repeat purchase. Once a pattern of purchase is established we describe the customer as brand loyal; the more cynical might describe this as addiction.

!!!

- Neither as a business person nor as a customer should you underestimate the potential power and influence of co-ordinated marketing activity. Smells, music and lighting can all be used to influence customer responses in retail environments.
- Marketing tools can be used for good or questionable ends. Each individual needs to make his or her own moral and ethical judgements about what is acceptable and what is not. For example, the same tools could (within the legal restrictions now imposed) be used to promote or discourage smoking. The individual manager must make his or her own choices.

Fig 8.3 Making customers less price sensitive

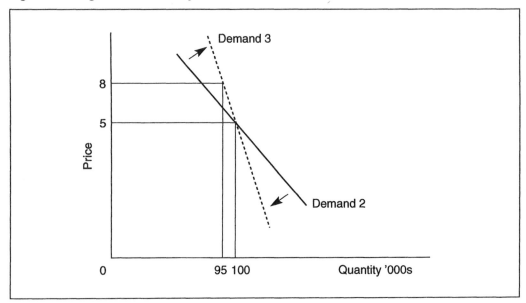

The marketing activity can therefore be employed not just to shift the demand curve but to alter its slope, making customers less price sensitive – see Fig. 8.3.

With a steeper demand curve, Demand 3, the price rise to 8 only results in a fall in demand of 5 per cent, or 5,000 units, increasing total revenues.

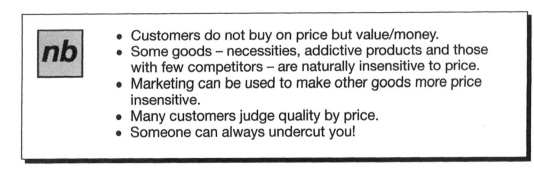

Matching customer demands
- Do not make the mistake of thinking that marketing is always about increasing sales. The real task of marketers is to ensure that there are enough customers to take up the organization's supply – in other words, to match demand and supply.
- Because the balance of demand and supply can vary over time and markets, the tactical tools of marketing have to be fine-tuned to achieve the objectives of matching demand and supply – tackling both peaks and troughs of demand.

Although the elements of the marketing mix are all detailed individually, like individual music scores for each instrument in an orchestra, it is in their combination that the skill of the marketing professionals should show. But if the organization is not committed to customer orientation, marketing will have only limited influence over most of the mix elements – so all will be 'playing' in isolation, a cacophony rather than a concert.

Product/service

What the customer is buying is the most obvious element of the marketing mix. Customer decisions will be potentially influenced by the range, style and presentation of the product. There are three dimensions that offer customer benefits, as shown in Fig. 8.4 (overleaf). All three dimensions generate benefits.

- Don't rely on functionality.
- Product/operationally oriented organizations tend to concentrate on functionality – what the product does. Certainly functionality is important to buyers, but these days it is a lack of functionality that would influence demand.
- The fact that a product or service works is expected – it is critical to remaining in business but no longer enough to earn you the necessary competitive advantage to keep you there.

Fig 8.4 The three dimensions of customer benefits

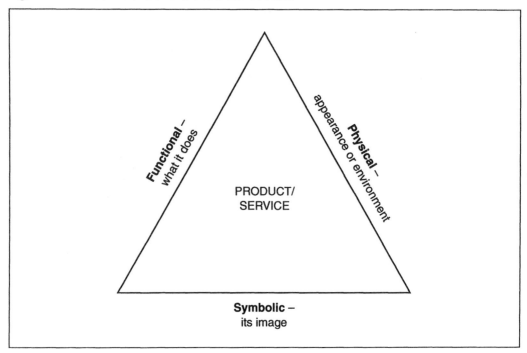

In the more affluent, advanced economies where customers have choice, it is the physical evidence and image of a product which are most likely to influence demand positively.

Kotler describes this as the total product concept – see Fig. 8.5 – recognizing that there are core and expected benefits, without which the customer would not consider you as a potential supplier. It is the augmented or differentiated benefits that can win you customer loyalty.

In the not-for-profit and public sectors functionality is often very good, but lack of investment in the environment has led to a poor, second-rate image. Accommodation and service, once seen as augmented benefits, are increasingly expected by a more affluent user base.

Fig 8.5 Total product concept

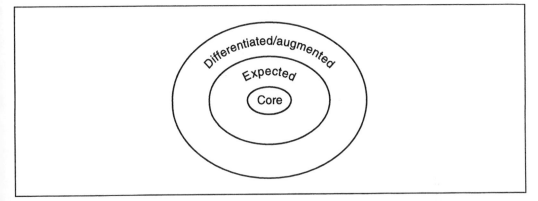

Price

We have already indicated some of the limitations of price as an influencer of demand, but in the marketing mix there are other dimensions which need consideration under the heading of price. Terms of payment can change a buyer's perception, as can discounts, loyalty bonuses and special

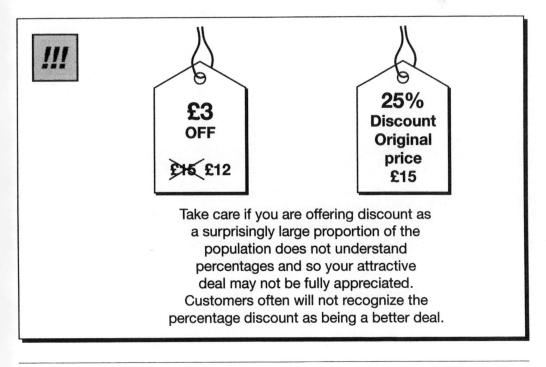

Take care if you are offering discount as a surprisingly large proportion of the population does not understand percentages and so your attractive deal may not be fully appreciated. Customers often will not recognize the percentage discount as being a better deal.

promotional offers. Tactical use of pricing can be very effective – for example, the £9.99 price tag is seen to be more attractive than £10.

The pricing challenge

- Who sets prices in your business?
- What methods are used?
- What input does marketing have?

Pricing is not a decision for marketers alone, but it is one they should be actively involved with. It is the most challenging decision the business must make. Get it badly wrong and you will have no business left:

- too high and customers will not buy
- too low and your costs will not be covered.

Given this vital importance to the very survival of the operation it is less than surprising that it is a decision which has often been left to the guardians of the firm's financial health – accountants. Neat pricing models based on cost-plus calculations have been approved of because they minimize risks in this sensitive area.

Marketers need to be very sensitive in how they approach the issue of price setting – price is the only element of the marketing mix which generates revenue, the others generate costs. It is not a decision which *any* functional specialists should be taking in isolation. Pricing decisions need to draw on information from across the whole organization.

The problem with pricing

The price/cost/volume relationship is the cause of the conundrum in price setting: the price will determine the quantity demanded – the volume. The total and average costs

Fig 8.6 Price/cost/volume relationship

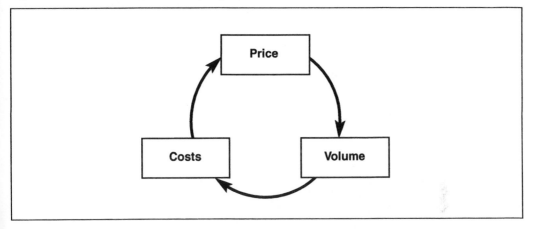

of the operation are determined by the volume produced, and the cost is fundamental to what price is charged. This is a vicious circle which is hard to break into – see Fig. 8.6.

Break-even analysis is a useful model for trying to examine the various pricing options and their impact on performance – see Fig. 8.7.

Fig 8.7 Break-even analysis

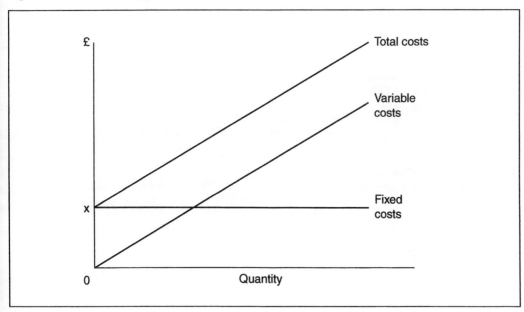

Fixed costs are those incurred by the business even if it was closed down for the month. These include rent, interest charges, salaries and wages, although these are more accurately semi-fixed costs as they can be changed through redundancy, part-time working, etc.

Variable costs are those which are incurred only when the business is operational – for example, casual staff wages, raw material costs, energy costs, and so on. They do not always work out as simply a constant £Y per unit produced, but will increase with output and are zero when the business is not operational.

Total costs are the important figure as these represent the minimum which must be earned if the business is to survive.

On to the chart of costs (Fig. 8.8), it is simple to plot a curve showing the total revenue if price were £Y or if it were £Z (price × quantity = total revenue).

Fig 8.8 The price/value curve

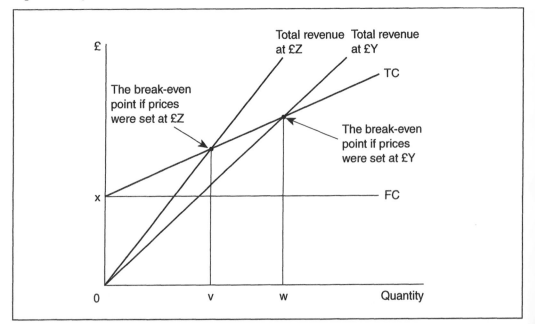

From this the manager can see that if they were to set prices at £Z they must sell V quantity in order to cover costs. Anything above sales of V will make a profit, below it a loss. The break-even graph below (Fig. 8.9) allows an easy calculation of how big that profit or loss might be.

Market-facing managers must now seek to forecast what volume of sales might actually be achieved if price were £Z. By repeating this demand forecast at the lower price of £Y the manager has a basis for assessing which price could be expected to yield the highest profits.

If you have the available financial information try to calculate the break-even point at a range of prices for one of your products or services.

Fig 8.9 Calculating profit and loss

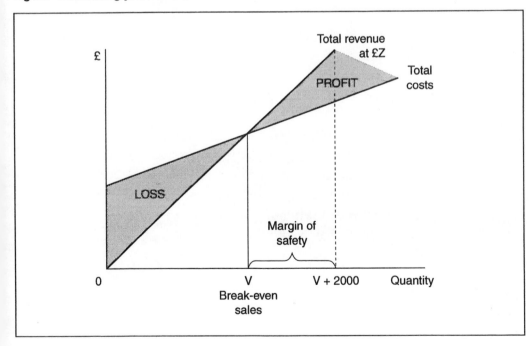

The object of the exercise is not, of course, to break even but to exceed break-even. If your demand forecast at £Z were V + 2,000 sales, the 2,000 would be your margin of safety – sales forecasts could be out by 2,000 units and you would still cover all your costs. The bigger the margin of safety the lower the risk.

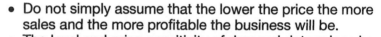

- Do not simply assume that the lower the price the more sales and the more profitable the business will be.
- The level and price sensitivity of demand determines how much is bought at any price – you need to go through the exercise for every product and market.

Marginal pricing

If a customer will not or cannot afford to pay the price set, but offers you a rate which is greater than the variable or marginal costs, should you accept it?

It might be tempting. The difference between the offered price and the marginal cost of producing that unit would be a contribution towards your fixed overheads costs, or, if you were past the break-even point, would represent increased profits.

In some sectors, marginal cost-based pricing is a common practice. Most notable is the service sector, where surplus capacity cannot be stockpiled. An empty bed in a hotel or a seat on an airline represents potential income lost forever. A last-minute booking looks attractive as an alternative, as long as the price exceeds the variable costs.

- If not used with care and carefully controlled it is possible that the total contributions above the variable costs fail to cover the fixed costs of the operation. This is not an approach to pricing generally favoured by accountants, unless accompanied by tight control policies.
- The different prices charged to your customers can cause dissatisfaction amongst the higher payers, who feel discriminated against. This loss of goodwill needs to be considered when you evaluate the cost/benefit of accepting business on a marginal cost basis.

The art of price setting

In practice, because there are so many variables which should be considered, price setting must be seen as a management art, not a science (see Fig. 8.10). Cost-based models, formulas and demand analysis can play a part, but in the end, in marketing the pricing decision, you must weigh up a number of variables.

Fig 8.10 Setting the price

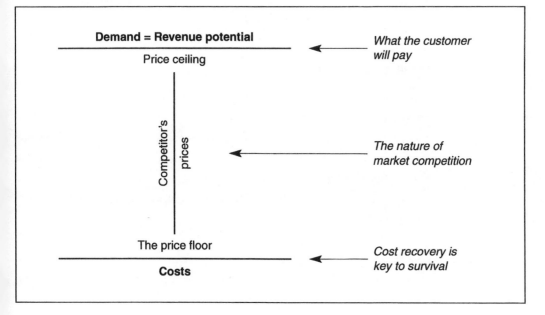

The broad parameters of price setting can be seen to be:

- the cost base
- the competitor's pricing strategies
- the customer.

The more of a buyer's market it is, i.e. the more competitive the market, the closer price will be to the price floor and the more susceptible to commoditization the market will be. The more of a seller's market it is, the closer prices can be to the price ceiling.

There are, however, other criteria which may influence pricing decisions:

- positioning of the business or brand
- price of other products in the range
- product-line pricing
- payment terms and loyalty schemes
- indirect taxes and surcharges
- promotional and tactical pricing opportunities
- customer's perceptions of value/money and quality
- the image of the business.

Public services and pricing

In some public and not-for-profit services, provision is free or heavily subsidized at the point of delivery. This means managers in these organizations have only 6Ps to influence demand levels, which makes their task harder. It also changes the user's, and often staff's, perceptions of service quality. 'Free' or 'cheap' is too often perceived to equal poor or second-rate service.

Users of the UK health or emergency services, education or community services often forget the indirect payments they have made through taxation and have little or no concept of the true price of a hospital visit or a month's schooling. With a perceived low quality image, poor service and customer care are often expected and eventually delivered. Morale of the staff is undermined because of the same low-value image of their work. A spiral of decline seems inevitable.

It might be a good idea if all users of public sector services received a bill indicating the true cost of their purchase, but indicating the contribution from local or central funds. For example, a mature student attending an evening class pro-gramme at a local college would get a bill like this:

$$
\begin{array}{rl}
£ & \\
1,000 & \text{– course and tuition fees} \\
\text{less } 750 & \text{– local authority contribution} \\
\hline
= \quad 250 & \text{– fee balance to pay}
\end{array}
$$

More aware of the true cost of his or her programme, this student is less likely to skip classes and more likely to demand punctuality and performance from the tutors.

Promotion

The subject of promotion and its planning is covered in detail in chapter 9, but we need here to consider its overall influence on customer demand and the customer's percep-tion of the value of a purchase.

Promotional activity adds value in several ways:

- it creates image – promotional activities produce the sym-bolic values associated with a purchase. The branding represents status or fashion, which sustains premium prices in the marketplace. Reebok trainers and Lacoste T-shirts, Chanel perfumes and Dior designs are all examples of this, but Coca-Cola, McDonald's and Mars also have established images that add to consumption values

- reputation reduces perceived risk – established product and company images reduce the customer's risk in purchase. Brands like Sony, IBM and Vidal Sassoon are world-renowned, safe and reliable. If there is a problem, you know it will be put right
- direct promotional value – some elements of the promotional activity more directly add value. Recipe cards on packaging, advice and customer information, sales promotions offering gifts or prizes, and even the carrier bags provided by retailers are functional as well as promotional
- promotion reassures – once a purchase decision has been made, customers may have second thoughts. This doubt reduces their satisfaction with the product – we refer to it as cognitive dissonance. Promotion post-purchase helps reassure buyers that they made a good decision and so ensures their continued satisfaction and retains their long-term customer loyalty.

Place

Place refers to the availability of a product or service – when and where it can be purchased. The price, particularly for a service, is not just the cash cost, but also covers the time involved in going to the dentist, bank or shopping centre. Many market segments are increasingly more time sensitive than price sensitive and so the contribution of 'place' to customers' satisfaction should not be underestimated.

How easy does your business make it to buy? How do your competitors do it differently? What can you learn from other business sectors? Take time to do some mystery shopping, to audit your own availability and to generate ideas for how you might add value to your operation with this variable.

A number of sectors are finding that they can gain considerable competitive advantage through changes in distribution. Technology has facilitated telephone banking and at-home shopping. Business to business firms are helping their clients lower stock holdings with just in time delivery services. Today you can have the benefit of home deliveries for a wide range of products and services.

Each of these examples demonstrates the extent to which today's customer values convenience, and is evidence of companies using this knowledge to win customers.

The extended service mix

The 4Ps we have considered so far – product, price, promotion and place – represent the original 4Ps of the marketing mix. Over time the special needs of services have led to an extension of the mix to 7Ps. The additional 3Ps – people, physical evidence and processes – are added specifically to help service managers deal with:

- intangibility of service
- inability to stockpile
- the contact between operational staff and customers, necessitated because production, distribution and consumption occur simultaneously.

Marketing a service is intrinsically no different from marketing a product, but these characteristics do make it hard and mean that:

- customers perceive a higher risk with services
- quality consistency is a problem
- customer care is a key issue because the customer is on your premises
- customers must be persuaded to give up time as well as cash.

- As technology makes it harder and harder for firms to compete on functionality so, increasingly, manufacturers see service as the added value which can enable them to win and sustain competitive advantage.
- The basis of relationship marketing rests on the firm's ability to offer customer service from consultancy to customer care. Therefore, whether your business involves products or services you might find extending your marketing mix to 7Ps will give you additional and perhaps innovative opportunities to influence demand.

People

In the delivery of a service it is the people who make the difference. Front-line staff – nurses, delivery drivers, waiters or receptionists – impact strongly and directly on the customer's perceptions of the service delivered. In a customer-oriented business, the following challenges must be met to make the most of your people:

- recruit the right staff
- provide them with the right skills
- empower them to tackle customer problems
- support them to make improvements in service delivery
- motivate them to care
- provide the back-up of management and systems to do the job right first time.

Effective customer service is dependent on people, and their importance to the customer should not be underestimated.

- Customer care is much more than training staff to smile and say 'have a nice day'. The quality of customer care is the responsibility of management, not a weakness which can be attributed to the front-line staff.
- Customer-oriented organizations value people – their customers outside and their employees inside. They respect and encourage everyone to treat colleagues as customers – the quality management approach.
- Valued staff lead almost inevitably to satisfied customers.

Physical evidence

What is the waiting room like at your local hospital? How is the college canteen furnished? Why do airlines have livery, staff uniforms and tickets which all reflect their corporate colours? You could be dropped into a McDonald's anywhere in the world and would recognize it from the strong primary colours, decor and physical evidence, all carefully created to support the McDonald's experience. Blindfolded, you would recognize Coca-Cola and Perrier by the shape of their bottles.

Physical evidence includes all the tangible evidence that reminds you of the product/service you are in the process of using up. In some services, like hotels and restaurants, the quality and cleanliness of the environment are critical to the positioning of the service.

These outward signs of service and quality impact strongly on customers. In the case of brochures and uniforms they play an important role in reducing perceived risk. Nurses, police and airline pilots all use uniforms to reassure those using their services. This reassurance can add immeasurably to the satisfaction level of the customer.

Processes

Processes are the systems and policies responsible for ensuring consistent quality of service provided. If you analyze your business you will find a series of interlinking systems all geared towards customer service. Your quality is only as good as the weakest link in that chain.

 Try tracking your systems from initial enquiry handling, through order processing to delivery, billing and complaint handling. How much value is added at each stage? What benefits do customers get from each process?

Action

The approach of 'value chain analysis' is based on this identification of each step and reviewing its role and contribution to customer satisfaction. This encourages managers to question and review traditional patterns of working, so helping identify opportunities for improvement.

In this chapter we have overviewed each of the elements of the marketing mix. For your plan you must now make a series of tactical decisions related to each of these. Figure 8.11 gives illustrative extracts from a tactical programme to achieve an agreed positioning of a 4-star service provider.

From this example you can see that the tactics are about change. They do not record the position now but detail what must be done to change it. Behind each tactical recommendation there may need to be a more detailed timetable and allocation of roles. Each identified manager would be

Fig 8.11 A tactical programme

	Product/service	By when?	Who?	£
1	Invest in redecoration of main reception areas	Completed by week 20	Manager A co-ordinates	50,000
	Promotion			
2	A revamped corporate identity, emphasizing quality appeal, to be produced and implemented across all materials	Completed week 52	Manager B	100,000
	Price			
3	Policy of price discounts and special deals to be discontinued	Now	All managers	—
4	Price points gradually repositioned up 15 per cent as upgrading is achieved	Completed week 52	Managing director co-ordinates	Lost business monitored
	Place			
5	A new 24-hour booking system installed	Installed by week 52	Booking supervisor	Annual cost 80,000
	Physical evidence			
6	New signing consistent with revamped corporate image	By week 30	Manager B	20,000
7	All conference delegates to receive branded leather folders	By week 26	Manager B	10 per head
8	All residents receive hospitality packs in rooms	By week 15	Manager A	6 per head
9	New staff uniforms to be selected with staff	By week 40	Design consultant	100,000
	People			
10	Staff training in operational and customer care areas to be implemented following appraisals and training needs assessment with all employees	All appraisals complete by week 26 Training on-going	All managers	500 p.a per staff member
	Processes			
11	All processes to be reviewed and report made of weaknesses and recommended areas for improvement	Completed week 16	Quality circles drawn from all staff	
12	Priority list for action	Week 18	Senior managers	250,000

responsible for producing this and accounting for progress in that area.

Tactical planning should help you make the transition from talking about the future, to taking positive steps, to bringing about your desired outcome. Remember the following about a tactical programme:

- some things will only get started in the year, e.g. staff training
- many areas will need to involve staff at all levels
- all things cannot be achieved at the same time
- including target dates and broad budget figures provides the starting point for controls (we will consider controls in more detail in chapter 10).

Use the proformas at the end of this chapter to help you begin the process of tactical planning. You will need to add to them and modify them for your own business, but once in place they will act as templates for next year, making the planning process easier.

- Do not try to achieve too much at once.
- Try producing tactical plans for six months to get you started.
- Review your progress regularly and make sure you have communicated both the intended programme and progress to all staff.

Proformas for tactical plans

	What?	By when?	Who?	£
Pricing				
Rates				
Discount policy				
Payment arrangements				
Other strategic considerations				

	What?	By when?	Who?	£
Place				
Location				
Availability				
Access				
Booking service				
Condition				
Opening				
Priority given				

	What?	By when?	Who?	£
Product				
Product range				
Quality				
Added-value services				
New products				
Promotion				
Objectives:				
– awareness				
– attitude				
– action				

	What?	By when?	Who?	£
Promotional strategy				
Target audience				
Benefits sought				
Promotional positioning				
Corporate brand				
Message				
Communication mix				
Control measures				

	What?	By when?	Who?	£
People				
Service level targets				
Customer care training				
Physical evidence				
• uniforms				
• environment				
• tickets/brochures, etc.				
•				
•				

CHAPTER 9

Effective communication

A guide to promotional planning

Marketers – the messengers

The communication process

Using the communication tools

The communication tools examined

The promotional plan

A guide to promotional planning

The term 'promotion' can be somewhat misleading. For many it seems to conjure up images of 'foot in the door' sales teams and manipulative messages aiming to get people to buy things they neither need nor want. This hard-sell activity, which certainly has been used by some sectors, has contributed to marketing getting a bad name with some people, but such tactics are in fact characteristic of non-customer-oriented companies. It is those organizations that are still operationally or sales oriented, producing goods they think customers want, that have to use strong persuasion techniques on customers.

A truly market-oriented operation needs only to communicate with the customer, informing rather than unduly influencing him or her. Certainly, persuasion will be in evidence, but more to demonstrate differences between products than to win unwilling purchasers. The shift from a transaction approach to a relationship focus for business is characteristic of the marketing influence which recognizes that promotional pressure may win a sale, but *not* a loyal customer.

A favourite simple definition of marketing is 'selling products that don't come back to customers who do'. It is this communication role of marketing which will be the focus of this chapter. We will examine:

- the communication responsibilities of the marketing function
- the position of selling
- the significance of the DMU and DMP in promotional planning
- the tools of communication and their strengths and weaknesses
- the production of a promotional plan.

Marketers – the messengers

The marketing function, as we have already identified, is often confused simply with the promotional activity. Sometimes this incorporates selling, while in other organizations sales is still mistakenly positioned separately.

Promotion in marketing terminology actually represents communication. The term 'promotion' has been so widely adopted because of the development of the 4Ps as a mnemonic for the marketing mix. The main role of marketing in a business is to act as the organization's messenger – taking messages back (market research) and forth (promotion) between the company and its customers. Our involvement with co-ordination of the other elements of the mix is because the price, packaging and distribution choices also send messages to the customer, and co-ordination of these messages is the responsibility of marketing.

★

- Marketing's expertise in message taking and sending should not be restricted to communication with customers. Its skills can be equally valuable when dealing with all stakeholder groups from shareholders to government departments.
- Many organizations are also adopting marketing planning techniques and expertise for the management of change and marketing of plans to their own staff (see the section in chapter 10 on internal marketing).

- Do not forget that one-way communication is a recipe for failure both with internal and external audiences.
- Open and effective communication channels are prerequisites for a responsive and successful organization, whatever its size.

The communication process

The actual communication process is simple, although there are many possible pitfalls. All managers will be familiar with the basics because they remain the same as for inter-personal communication. They are simple enough: there must be a sender and a receiver – see Fig. 9.1. Not much can go wrong here, you might think.

The next requirement is the message – see Fig. 9.2. What is the purpose of the communication? Too few managers still take the

Fig 9.1

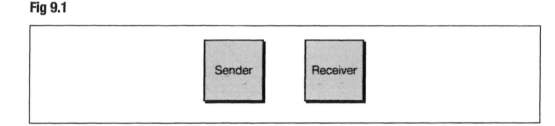

Fig 9.2

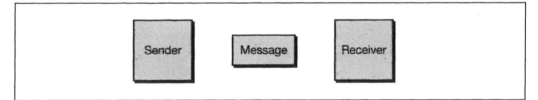

time to think through carefully their communication objectives, which results in inappropriate messages being developed.

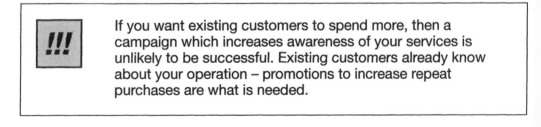

If you want existing customers to spend more, then a campaign which increases awareness of your services is unlikely to be successful. Existing customers already know about your operation – promotions to increase repeat purchases are what is needed.

- Even before communication begins, the receiver may have a preconceived, inaccurate or unhelpful image of the sender. What are the implications if the receiver is labelled as an American organization or a British company, a youngster or a professional? The image of the sender will impact on the weight the receiver places on any message received.
- The sender may have set his or her sights on the wrong receiver. Perhaps the segmental analysis was poor or the wrong person in the decision-making unit (DMU) has been targeted.

Once you know what you want to say, then you need to decide how best to say it. The message needs 'encoding' – putting into words, symbols and images in a way that the audience will receive and interpret in the spirit, and with the meaning, intended (see Fig. 9.3).

Fig 9.3

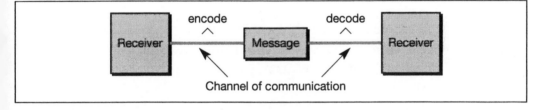

- Take time to test out any and all communication messages with a sample drawn from your target audience. From your brochures and sales letters to advertisements and answerphone messages, all communication needs decoding and the receiver's response will be to tone, style and presentation as much as to the words used.
- Take particular care when working across international audiences as culture most strongly impacts on decoding.

- It is easy when planning communication to be lured into the big, glossy approach.
- Whilst all communication needs to be professional and consistent with the overall image and positioning of the business, an informal meeting can often achieve as much with a closely defined audience as can reams of letters and glossy brochures.

The message developed must also be appropriate for the channel of communication selected – for example, the content of a brochure would not translate well into letter format and a press release would need adapting for a telesales presentation. The channel of communication also needs selecting with care if your message is to reach the intended audience in a cost-effective way.

The problem of noise

Communication does not, unfortunately, take place in a vacuum or even, sadly, a quiet place. Noise of all types is likely to distract your audience – see Fig. 9.4. It might literally be external noises, but it is more likely to be distractions caused by other activities, such as making tea during the commercial break. Noise is also generated by competitor activities and claims – conflicting messages confuse the receiver, who is likely to respond by ignoring both.

- Critical to successful communication is its ability to be heard despite the noise.
- Messages need to grab and retain audience interest. Make a point of noticing those that achieve this for you. How effective is your own communication?

Fig 9.4

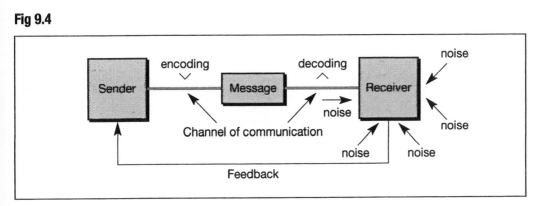

Feedback

The final element of the communication process is feedback. Ask yourself the following questions:

- Did the communication work?
- Did the right message get to the right person?
- Was it received and understood?
- Was it acted upon?
- How could it be improved?

Promotion and communication activities are resource-hungry. Feedback is essential to the constant challenge of improving the efficiency and effectiveness of the business – see Fig. 9.5 (overleaf). Audits will help you to identify causes of communication problems and allow you to learn from the last campaign's successes and failures.

The DMU and DMP

In earlier chapters we have considered both the decision-making process (DMP) and the decision-making unit (DMU). Understanding both is key to successful communication activity and so they are worth revisiting here.

The DMU
Organizations are likely to be faced with a multiplicity of possible audiences for their communication activities. Customers,

Fig 9.5 Ensuring promotional efficiency and effectiveness

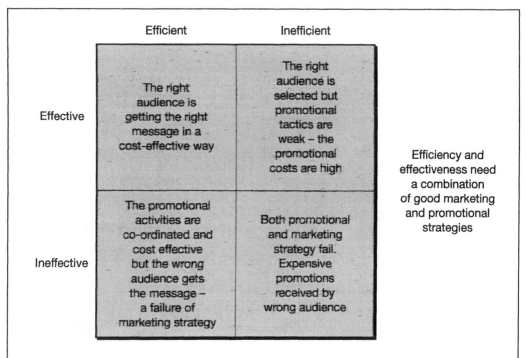

consumers, decision-makers, advisers and financiers may all
have a part to play in the purchase decision. So, who should the
promotional activity focus upon? The mistake is to fail to recognize these various audience groups and to broadcast a single
message irrespective of their role in the DMU and taking no
account of the differences in their needs and motives.

Marketers need to research their own DMU in some depth to
establish:

- who is involved
- their needs
- their relative influence/importance.

In practice the promotional plan will not be a one-
dimensional activity. A combination of activities will be
orchestrated to deliver appropriate benefit-oriented mes-

sages to all the constituent parts of the DMU. For example, a computer equipment company may use:

- public relations, executive briefings and direct mail to draw the attention of key corporate decision-makers
- exhibitions, brochures and demonstrations to influence the views of consultants, IT managers and other advisers
- sales pitches, workplace demos and hospitality to influence the official buyers and, possibly, end-users.

The DMP

All the aforementioned groups need to be moved through the decision-making process (DMP), although they may not all be at the same place on it at the same time.

The DMP recognizes that action, be that sales, a vote cast or donation given, will only happen after the audience has been made aware and convinced that the action is beneficial to him or her. The audience must shift from:

Unawareness → Awareness → Attitude → Action

It is possible to break these steps down further. Attitude is sometimes divided into interest and desire (although it is not always easy to identify and separate these states), and trial is sometimes included between attitude and action. Whichever way you choose to break down the buying process in your sector the different staging posts give you a framework for analyzing the current promotional activities and for setting future objectives.

Objective setting

Promotional objectives must be broken down to reflect the DMP stages. They need to be set in terms of:

- awareness
- attitude
- action.

Do not make the mistake of trying to judge the success of your promotional activity as an integrated whole. Whilst you will be able to see that a promotional spend of, say, £50,000 resulted in 500 sales – a promotional cost of £100 per sale – it gives you no basis for evaluating the effectiveness of the promotional activities at each stage of the DMP.

As an example, £50,000 was spent as follows and generated the following results:

- £30,000 spent on advertising generated 5,000 enquiries
- 5,000 brochures were dispatched, generating 1,000 requests for a quote – each brochure cost £3 to dispatch (£15,000)
- 1,000 telephone quotes were given at a cost of £5 each.

In this example it is possible to identify interest (brochure request) and desire (quote request).

The more detailed breakdown in Fig. 9.6 gives you much more sense of the effectiveness of the promotional activity. Say you wanted to increase sales by another 250, you could look to increase promotional spending by £25,000 and would know to have 2,500 brochures available, the capacity to handle 500 quotes and the goods to satisfy the 250 orders. Alternatively, you could examine ways of getting more from

Fig 9.6 Tracking promotional effectiveness

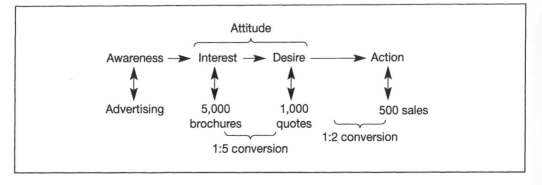

less. You could ask how conversion rate from enquiries to quotations could be improved:

- does the brochure promote the right benefits?
- are its messages effectively encoded?
- could promotional offers, such as a prize draw entry for all who request a quote, increase quotation requests?

The sales conversion from quotations might be examined, though it is not bad at 1:2 – but improved techniques might perhaps get it higher.

- Before increasing the numbers who are aware and interested through expensive advertising activities, why not review the customer database? Mailshot those who enquired or asked for a quote last year. Their lack of purchase may have been a postponement not a decision to buy elsewhere.
- Their key to good planning lies in the quantification.
- Once you have numbers (however crude they are at first), you have mechanisms for setting objectives and monitoring performance which are the keys to improved efficiency.

Setting an objective in the above example of a 1:4 quotation from brochure rate (a 20 per cent improvement) whilst maintaining the sales conversion at 1:2 would lead to an additional 125 sales – a 25 per cent improvement – and average promotional costs would have fallen.

Using the communication tools

As already indicated, the marketer has available a range of communication tools, and the selection of which to use in what combination needs to be done with care and consideration. The different communication methods work more or less effectively at the various stages of the decision-making process. For example, advertising, with its mass media message, is excellent for generating awareness and stimulating interest but much less powerful when it comes to the all-important generation of action.

Personal selling on the other hand is so powerful at generating action that in the UK legislation exists to protect individuals from the persuasiveness of the enthusiastic insurance and double glazing salesperson, by allowing a seven-day cooling-off period after a contract is signed.

In the model shown in Fig. 9.7 you can see how the various promotional techniques relate in terms of effectiveness. The lines indicate only the general direction and strength of effect at each stage but are not plotted against a specific quantified scale.

Fig 9.7 An overview of the effectiveness of communication tools

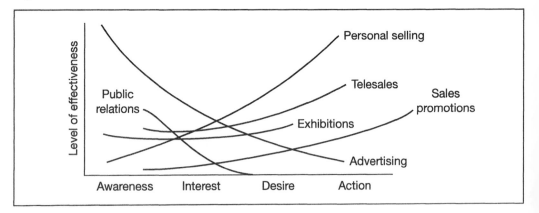

The communication tools examined

Advertising

A variety of mediums for advertising exist, including television, newspapers, magazines, posters, radio, and more unusual channels like parking meters and taxis. The limitation of advertising is that it is still essentially one-way communication with a standardized message, broadcast to a wide audience. However, the proliferation of TV channels and magazine titles does provide the advertiser with more opportunity to segment the audience and tailor messages more specifically. At the same time the rapid development of interactive channels and sales presenter technology will from now on erode the fundamental weakness of one-way communication messages.

- Do not make the mistake of forgetting that advertising media should be selected on the basis of the match between their audience profile and your target market segment.
- The cost per thousand messages received may seem cheaper with a different title, but if your message is not seen by the 'right' 1,000 people it will in the long run be an expensive waste of effort.
- Media buyers must buy space not on price alone but on the basis of value for money from every promotional pound.

Personal selling

This element of the communications mix is not only the most powerful in generating action, but also the most expensive. Big budgets in advertising terms pale into insignificance when the cost per call of a field sales team is calculated. The task of the marketing manager is to treat the sales team as a limited resource and maximize its impact through support activities and systems.

A programme of exhibition activities could generate qualified sales leads, as could a telesales support team. Improved training and sales support materials can help get more from less sales effort. Remember that anyone in direct customer contact is a sales person for the organization and will require similar skills and training.

- It is still not uncommon, particularly in the business to business sector, for sales and marketing activities to be split into different functional departments, with limited communication between the two.
- There can be no question that the activities of the sales effort must be co-ordinated and integrated with the rest of the promotional and marketing efforts – they must, therefore, be orchestrated by marketing. This has unfortunately become seen as a hierarchical issue instead of a planning one.

Effective sales skills are critical to a successful organization. They must be valued and supported, but nonetheless need to be incorporated into the overall promotional plan – see Fig. 9.8.

It is important to remember the real costs of a field sales force – effective selling time can be very limited once travel, preparation and waiting times are taken into consideration. Using telesales support teams to take repeat orders and retain routine contact with clients, so reducing sales call frequency, is one way you may be able to make better use of your valuable sales resource.

Sales promotions

Temporary changes in the elements of the marketing mix can be used to 'promote sales'. Normally used tactically, promotions can help convert awareness into action – for example, when you launch a new product or build relationships by increasing repeat purchases or visits.

Sales promotion is a powerful tool when employed creatively and appropriately. Sales promotions should be combined within the overall communication activity and developed to support sales activities and to add impact to advertising campaigns. The offers made must appeal directly to the target audience and be perceived by them to add

Fig 9.8 Organizing the sales and marketing activities

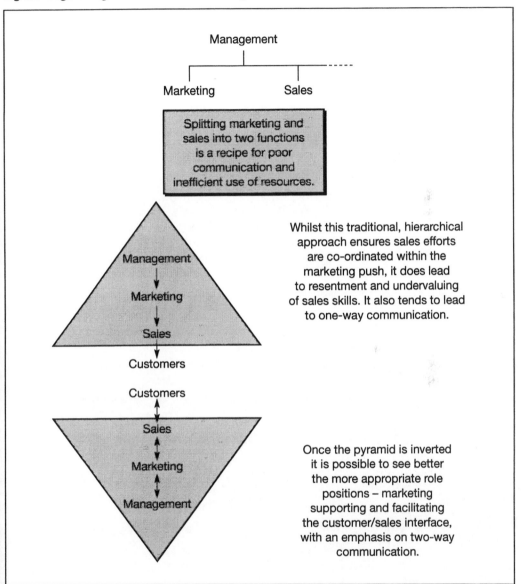

value. A 'money off' offer will have limited appeal to a price-insensitive segment, and free gifts or potential prizes need to reflect the quality and image of the brand.

- It is all too easy to think up an idea for a sales promotion before identifying the objective. The result is a programme of ad hoc creative events which play no integrated part in the achievement of the specified communication and marketing objectives.
- Used in an unco-ordinated way, promotional offers and events can add interest and variety for the customer but will fail to maximize the benefit to the organization.

- Legislation and voluntary controls are complex in the area of sales promotion. Advice and information before developing a promotion can avoid the possible costs and damage to image if a promotion is challenged.
- Copies of the sales promotion code of practice and advice from practitioners are available free from the Advertising Standards Authority in the UK, at:

Brook House
2–16 Torrington Place
London WC1E 7HN

020 7580 5555

A checklist for developing sales promotion

The audit
- What is the stage for the product life cycle?
- What are the communication objectives?
- What are the brand values and agreed positioning?
- Who are the target audience and what are their needs and preferences?
- What is the history of sales promotions activities for this product/company?
- What other communication activities are planned?

Set objectives
- Establish clear, quantified sales promotion objectives set over time.

Develop strategy
- Brainstorm possible sales promotion activities to help achieve the objective.
- Select the option which is best suited to the needs of the customers and the organization. Check it in terms of:
  - image
  - logistical implications
  - cost
  - integration with the rest of the mix
  - perceived value by the customer
  - conformity with relevant codes of practice.

Establish feedback
- Determine how the promotion will be assessed and establish feedback mechanisms.

Implementation
- Source any necessary gifts or merchandise.
- Brief all those involved or affected, including sales teams and distributors.
- Co-ordinate other elements of the communication mix.
- Establish and communicate a promotion timetable.

---

eg | **McDonald's gets its kicks from Route 66**
In 1995 McDonald's developed and implemented its very successful 'Route 66' promotion for the UK. This is a good example of how promotions should be integrated with the whole communication and marketing mix if they are to achieve maximum impact. The promotion, offering a series of special meals based on locations along the famous Route 66, built on the exciting American image designed to boost purchases from young adults. A series of *Thelma and Louise* TV commercials was supported by point-of-sale displays and Route 66 background music in-store, and the chance to win holidays to the USA.

Public relations

Public relations (PR) is frequently seen as a Cinderella in the communications mix. Perceived incorrectly as 'free' it is too often treated only as an afterthought, of limited value. In fact, publicity, because it is judged by the audience to be objective, is often highly effective communication. However, like the other communication elements, PR requires investment of time and effort if it is to be successful or effective.

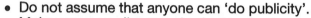

- Do not assume that anyone can 'do publicity'.
- Make sure you allocate a budget and set up mechanisms to measure the effectiveness of PR.
- Make sure you identify PR angles at the planning stage of all communication and business activities.
- Do not send out press releases exclusively about the 'sold out' successes rather than the 'coming soon' offers.

Publicity is not free: it costs to employ professional PR support, invite and entertain the media, set up activities or just to have photos taken and dispatched. Ultimately, all your efforts may go unrewarded if your event fails to get a mention in the right media, because publicity, unlike advertising, cannot be controlled. You cannot simply book space and insert your message; you must influence editors and journalists to take up your story or try your product.

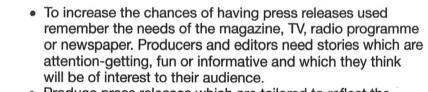

- To increase the chances of having press releases used remember the needs of the magazine, TV, radio programme or newspaper. Producers and editors need stories which are attention-getting, fun or informative and which they think will be of interest to their audience.
- Produce press releases which are tailored to reflect the interests of each publication, and always include photographs or an offer of an interview where possible.
- Keep press releases short and informative, and clearly indicate the source and an enquiries number.

It is worth developing contacts with journalists in your area, whether on the local paper and radio station, or in the trade press relevant to your business. Talk through forthcoming activities and events with them in advance. Often the 'behind the scenes' coverage will prove much more attractive than the formal and posed photocall opportunities. Offer each publication a unique angle and try to emphasize dimensions of particular interest to its audience.

- Always have a camera loaded with black and white film available to snap a shot of an unusual event, celebrity customer or any other newsworthy item.
- Work with suppliers and customers to identify opportunities for joint promotional stories like the signing of a new contract or opening of a newly refurbished store.
- Encourage your staff to identify PR opportunities, as the best stories will inevitably come from those in direct contact with customers. Set up systems so these can be responded to quickly.

- Every now and then some unfortunate event generates bad publicity. This is not the time for management to put their heads in the sand – it is unlikely to just 'go away'.
- You should be prepared in advance for such an eventuality. Identify a spokesperson and try to help the media by detailing the actions you have taken to rectify or mitigate the problem. Established media contacts are useful in helping you ensure that your views are heard.
- The damage of media coverage of a 'bad news' story can be considerably diminished if the problem can be demonstrated to have been tackled fairly and quickly.

A garden centre sows a few seeds

A small local garden centre, Phoebes of Catford, was prepared with its camera when flash floods hit the area. Along with many homes its greenhouse store area went under feet of water. On the front pages of the local papers that week were pictures of happy uniformed and badged staff sweeping water out of the store. For a local business, with an off-high street site and low local awareness, such coverage helped significantly with raising the profile of the store in the local community.

Exhibitions and displays

In certain business to business markets, exhibitions are a central element of the communications activity. With relatively small and easily identifiable customer bases, industry events provide cost-effective opportunities to meet buyers and demonstrate new products. These showcases do however require considerable effort. It is not simply a question of booking space and sending along a representative. Stands

!!!

- Do not make the mistake of trying to economize on staffing. Once you have committed yourself to attending an exhibition then you must be properly represented. Too few staff to cover the volume of visitors and inadequate staff breaks mean that not only will leads be lost, but also staff who are tired will find it hard to be motivated or caring of prospects they do meet.
- Keep stands looking professional – avoid clutter and the dirty coffee cup look. If you are overstaffed send people away for an hour or staff will outnumber visitors – a daunting prospect for any potential buyer.
- Do not measure the success of an exhibition by direct sales. Few companies should be using exhibitions to sell. Their purpose is to create awareness and generate interest. Qualified leads and an extension of the prospects database are more realistic objectives. Monitor future sales from those leads, but exhibition objectives should really be presented in terms of qualified leads gained.

must be staffed adequately with competent organizational representatives who are well trained in how to work in an exhibition environment.

Weighing up the costs and benefits

Whilst quantification of prospects and eventual sales is central to effective feedback from exhibitions, the less tangible benefits of renewed contact with existing customers should not be overlooked. In a similar way it is easy to forget the hidden costs of exhibition attendance – for example, the lost sales calls associated with taking staff away from their routine sales activities.

Direct mail

With improved technology and database management, the opportunity of direct mail should not be overlooked. Mail lists can be purchased easily, and sending brochures, offers and information to targeted groups can be a cost-effective way of generating awareness. Linked to sales promotions, direct mail can encourage clients to try a product – for example, to test drive a new car or request a quotation. Effective management of your own database can provide a cost-efficient means of informing clients of new products, etc. Improved technology is helping data warehousing and management.

!!! Customers are on the receiving end of 'junk mail' in enormous quantities. Make certain that any material you send is professionally produced, attention grabbing and details benefits, not just features.

Merchandising and point-of-sale

Whenever customers or clients come into your premises there is the opportunity for merchandising and point-of-sale techniques to be used to support the communication efforts. Well developed in retail, these tools are used relatively little in other environments and represent missed communication opportunities for many organizations.

 Walk into your premises as a customer. Go to reception or enquiries and look around – now go to the waiting room. Are company products and information displayed? Are the messages clear and co-ordinated or a random selection of framed publicity shots?

Advertising on the Internet, faxed promotional offers and interactive TV ads are all examples of how we can expect communication tools to improve and opportunities to grow. As a marketer your task is to keep aware of the available options and be able to evaluate the strengths and weaknesses of each in terms of creating awareness, generating interest, holding attention, changing attitude and completing sales for your business.

The promotional plan

Once you have considered all the elements you are in a position to pull them together as a coherent plan, scheduled over time. As a written document the promotional plan should follow exactly the same structure as the business and marketing plans, as follows:

- Where are we now?
- Where are we going?
- How do we get there?
- Who does what, when?
- Are we on the right track?

Where are we now?

The promotional audit will generate background which should give information on current levels of awareness and sales, as well as customer attitudes to the company/product. The marketing strategy, i.e. which customer segment is targeted, what positioning is required and who in the DMU is the intended audience, should be laid out.

Where are we going?

Clear objectives expressed against awareness, attitude and action are needed.

How do we get there?

The promotional strategy explains the balance of communication tools to be employed.

Who does what, when?

The detail of tactical promotional tasks must be co-ordinated to ensure synergy of effort across all mediums used in a campaign.

Are we on the right track?

Besides the detailed timetable, which can be used to check off progress against the plan, there should also be established feedback mechanisms and measures. Audited benchmarks of awareness and attitude pre-campaign can be compared with measures taken during and post-campaign. Recall research and enquiry levels can be used during a campaign. Both formal and informal methods can be used to capture the necessary feedback data. This information is invaluable in helping managers to plan their next campaign, as well as alerting them to weaknesses in the current plan.

About the budget

Many variations of method for setting a promotional budget have been used, but they fail to recognize the cause and effect relationship between promotional activity and customer behaviour. *Competitive parity* is one such model: it ignores your objectives and instead sets a budget based on an industry average or norm. This collective wisdom approach is questionable when all key players adopt the same approach.

'What can we afford?' This is another, not uncommon approach, allocating an annual budget as a sort of token or sacrifice rather than basing it on what we *need* to spend.

'Last year's plus a bit.' This similarly fails to take account of this year's circumstances – what do we want to achieve now and what is today's environment like?

Percentage of sales method. This takes last year's overall sales and allocates 2, 3 or 4 per cent of that as a budget for this year. This seems to assume that the sale comes before the promotional spend and so also does not help establish the cause and effect relationship clearly.

Better is the approach of taking the overall objective in revenue terms and calculating budget as a percentage of that. This treats promotion as a kind of marginal cost but fixed at x per cent of revenue.

- Percentage of sales is still not an ideal method of setting a promotional objective. It can, however, be a useful guide for establishing a likely budget total and for assessing current promotional spends. There are no hard and fast rules and the appropriate level is influenced by the stage of the life cycle, the nature of the sector and the current level of activity.
- In broad terms, spending between 1.5 and 6 per cent of targeted revenue would be an expected benchmark zone. For example, a mature business to business product needing to retain customer interest might need only 1.5 per cent but a growing consumer product seeking to expand its customer base could need 6 per cent.

Ultimately, the best method is the one which asks what are the needed promotional outcomes, how will we achieve these and how much will this cost? Using this objective and task method, the promotional inputs are clearly recognized as generating a desired outcome – cause and effect are understood. The communications team can now request and justify a budget allocation, thus ensuring a bottom-up as well as top-down dimension to the planning process.

Using external agencies

Most organizations, whatever their size, will use the services of external agencies in the production and implementation of promotional campaigns. Their brief, like that of the research agency, must be specific and provide all the detailed understanding of the segment and its behaviour and preferences. Choosing an appropriate agency is an important activity because you would expect to work with the same one over a number of campaigns.

Checklist for agency selection
- Does it offer the range of services you need?
- Does it have the geographic coverage you need?
- Does it know about your product or customers?
- Has it any conflicts of interest?
- How successful is it?
- Do you like the people?
- Is the agency commercially sound and organizationally reliable?
- How important would your business be to the agency?

Promotional plans need to be logically structured in the same way as the plans at other stages in the planning hierarchy. It is easy to waste promotional resources, so feedback and careful analysis of the effectiveness of activities are critical to removing the guesswork from promotional activities.

CHAPTER 10

Implementation and control

Making plans work

Winning support

Motivating the implementers

What is internal marketing?

Controlling plans

Monitoring performance

The budget

Closing the loop

Making plans work

Preparing plans is not in itself a particularly taxing exercise; it requires some preparation and thought but is essentially a simple process. The real test of the manager lies in the implementation of plans. Many, perhaps even the majority of, managers see the annual planning process as little more than a hoop-jumping exercise devised by senior management to keep them on their toes. There is little, if any, sense of the dynamic and continuous nature of the planning. Plans are fixed and, in the main, a paperwork activity. There is no obvious link between what appears in the plan and the actions taken over the following weeks. In small businesses planning is more likely to be one of those tasks for which there is never enough time. Any sense of managing future outcomes exists only in isolation in the partners' heads.

The implementation stage is the step that is critical to the success of the planning activity. If this part does not work then the whole effort will have been wasted. It is for that reason that you should take particular pains when planning the implementation stage.

In this chapter we will consider the following ingredients of effective implementation and control:

- winning support from colleagues and senior managers
- motivating and involving those who will implement the plan
- techniques of internal marketing
- converting the plans into a dynamic reference document
- the three elements of control – information, time and costs
- techniques for monitoring the effectiveness of marketing activity
- the importance of control in future planning.

Winning support

So far you have a plan that exists only on paper. You have a preferred strategy decided and you know what resources you need to achieve your objectives. Others may now need to be persuaded that your judgement is sound and that the plan is likely to bear fruit. This may involve senior managers being faced with competitive bids for resources from different strategic business units, it may be fellow partners undecided about further investment, or a bank manager whose support is required.

No matter whose support is needed the plan cannot be adopted without it, so the first stage in implementation is to win this support. The approach is to treat the stakeholders as customers and the plan as a product you want to market to them. In this way all the tools and frameworks, tips and techniques of marketing planning can be used to win over the audience. This is the concept of 'internal marketing'.

You can begin with some research. You may ask, who must be persuaded and what is their current attitude and past experiences, and who are the competitors for their support and what are their strengths and weaknesses? You may look into the needs of your audience by asking the following:

- Are they risk takers or risk averse?
- Do they want innovation or prefer tried and tested options?
- What returns over what time frames are necessary?
- What guarantees, security or evidence can you offer in support of your strategy?
- Who are the key influence and decision-makers in this DMU?

Once you have completed your investigations and analysis you will be better placed to present your proposals in a customer-oriented way, offering benefits if your plan is adopted which are valued by them.

A customer-oriented approach to internal customers recognizes that their needs are related to the outcomes rather than the processes or products used to achieve them. Justify your decisions in terms of specific outcomes wherever possible. The wrong thing to say would be: 'This new ABC widget is sure to be a winner with the customers because it is functionally better than its nearest competitor.' The right thing to say would be: 'Adding functionality to ABC widget will give us a competitive advantage that we forecast will help us increase market share by 5 per cent and add £1 million to our bottom-line profit by 2005.' You can see from the preceding statements that it would be much harder to reject latter cause if it were used to support a request for £250,000 of investment in ABC widget.

Always present

Sending in a written report to the management for consideration is rather like sending a brochure to a customer – it will probably generate awareness and interest but is much less likely to stimulate action. A presentation, on the other hand, has the power of the personal sales call. Objections can be handled, buying signals observed and responded to, and the sale of your proposal closed.

Therefore, whenever you are trying to win support for a plan try to also gain management's attendance at a presentation. Even if you are only facing a bank manager or single colleague, set up a form of presenter to take them through the key aspects and elements of the proposals.

 Many people find the idea of presenting in any environment too daunting to try to seek such an opportunity willingly. It is a mistake to give in to this nervousness because planned carefully the presentation will be easy and relatively painless, but the outcome will be the support you were seeking.

A presentation checklist

Select a venue and layout suitable for the audience – try to avoid confrontation across barriers like a desk, or from behind a rostrum. You will get more support if you can get into your audience's space. In both the layouts in Fig. 10.1 there is a physical barrier between you and the audience. By seating an audience around an open 'U' as in Fig. 10.2 you can enter their space – this removes the perceived barrier and comes across as positive body language. Moving to the side of the desk as in Fig. 10.3 (overleaf) also stops acting as a barrier to communication.

Fig 10.1

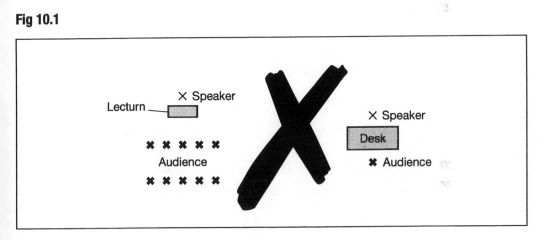

Fig 10.2

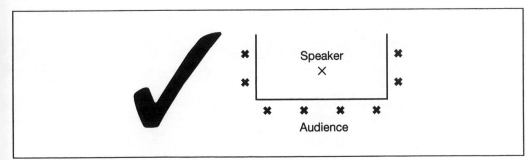

Fig 10.3

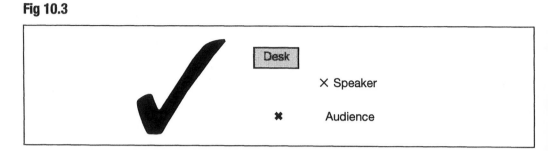

Plan what your message is carefully, bearing in mind the needs of the audience. Keep reminding yourself of what you want them to hear and what you want them to do. Use these two reminders as criteria for checking on the validity of each element of your presentation.

Plan how best to 'encode' your message. Use a series of visuals for maximum effect. These can be produced on overhead transparencies, on flipchart paper or as a written document, like a handout booklet for each member of the audience. In preparing and making your presentation you should try to:

- keep the wording short, with a summary of the key points. You will be able to elaborate on each as you take the audience through them
- wherever possible add charts, graphs, etc. to present numerical information. In Fig. 10.4 there are too many figures and the audience is left to do its own calculations – they will then lose track of what you are saying. Presented as a graph – see Fig. 10.5 – the buoyant sales forecast is clear to the audience; but remember that changing the scale of the axes changes the steepness of your graph. Choose a scale that suits your audience, be they ambitious or conservative, risk takers or risk avoiders
- keep the format and style similar across all the slides, and use colour and lots of white space to generate a professional and confident image

- keep spelling out the justification in terms of the benefits of your proposal
- take the audience through the logical steps, filling them in on background and leading them through objectives and strategy. Do not give them too much tactical detail as it will tend to confuse the picture. End with a clear statement of what is needed from them
- avoid cramming too much in. You should not need more than one visual for every one or two minutes of presentation. Experienced presenters may need fewer.

Once your presentation framework is prepared, practise your presentation. If you are nervous ask for questions at the end of the session. Prepare reminder notes on index cards

Fig 10.4

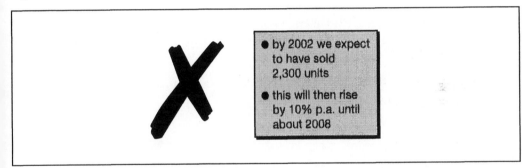

Fig 10.5

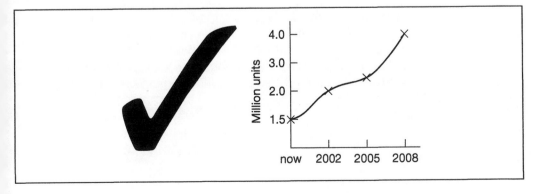

and put them in order, fixed with a treasury tag so you cannot shuffle them out of order. With practice you will find you can rely on the visuals as prompts and work without reference to your notes.

Try to do a run-through in the actual venue so you can check that you know how to operate any equipment like the overhead projector. Check the timing.

On the day keep any nerves at bay by arriving in plenty of time, breathing deeply and having all your necessary support materials ready. Start on time and tell the audience the objective of the presentation, outlining how long it will take and what you will be telling them. The golden rules of any presentation structure hold good here:

- *introduction* – tell them what you are going to tell them
- *middle* – tell them
- *conclusion* – tell them what you have told them.

Have written, formal report copies available to supplement your presentation.

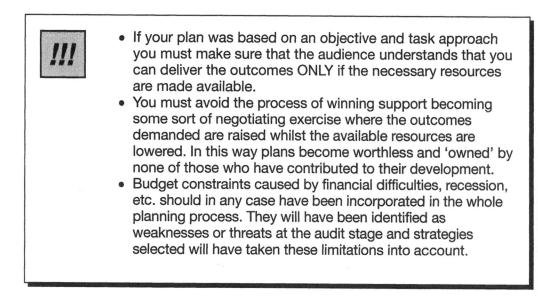

- If your plan was based on an objective and task approach you must make sure that the audience understands that you can deliver the outcomes ONLY if the necessary resources are made available.
- You must avoid the process of winning support becoming some sort of negotiating exercise where the outcomes demanded are raised whilst the available resources are lowered. In this way plans become worthless and 'owned' by none of those who have contributed to their development.
- Budget constraints caused by financial difficulties, recession, etc. should in any case have been incorporated in the whole planning process. They will have been identified as weaknesses or threats at the audit stage and strategies selected will have taken these limitations into account.

Motivating the implementers

Once a plan has approval the next step in its implementation requires the involvement of all those likely to be responsible or affected by its implementation.

 Do not make the mistake of only recognizing those immediately involved – for example, the sales team in the case of a new product launch. The customer service staff, PR department and suppliers may all be on the receiving end of customer enquiries. Distribution and logistics will need to know about delivery specifications, whilst finance may be faced with an increase in new customer accounts or special pricing arrangements for the launch.

Many of those charged with implementation will, it is hoped, have already contributed to the planning process, providing input to the audits and ideas for strategy and tactics. However, this stage is likely to involve a larger and potentially more diverse audience than at the first stage, so segmentation of the audience may be necessary. The process, however, is the same as at stage one:

- identify the audience segment and their needs, what they want to know and what their concerns might be
- develop an appropriate message relevant to the audience's needs and determine the best method of delivery – for example, a team meeting, personal briefing, sales conference, bulletin board or staff newsletter
- prepare and practise the presentation, and establish a programme to ensure all key segments receive the message at around the same time.

- If the plan requires considerable change to those who will be implementing it, appropriate benefits of that change must be spelt out or devised. For example, the distributor may be encouraged to change by the promise of higher sales volumes or preferential service, but the telesales team asked to alter their working patterns to extend the opening times for bookings may need financial incentives, or increased time off to encourage change.
- It is important to think through the implications of changes before presenting the plan to staff – they will certainly identify any issues quickly and will want answers to their concerns there and then.

What is internal marketing?

Selling your plan to both senior managers and operational teams represent examples of internal marketing. Because successful implementation is impossible without their support and co-operation it makes sense to spend time and effort to ensure this is won. If you apply the frameworks, techniques and concepts of marketing to influencing the behaviour and actions of an internal audience, you are involved with internal marketing.

How much internal marketing will be necessary depends on the size of the internal planning gap – i.e. the difference between, for example, the resources management might expect to give you and what you need for this project, or the current working conditions and what they will be after the

If your plans are not adopted by management, consider your own role in selling and presenting the proposal to them effectively. Are you presenting relevant benefits to them and recognizing the cost of proposals in terms of risk or alternative opportunities forgone? Do not blame them for their lack of foresight before you have reviewed your own marketing skills.

change. The degree of risk, amount of change or resources needed are the key considerations when thinking about internal marketing.

An internal marketing plan and strategy

The internal business objective set should be as clear and quantified as any other objective. For example, you may want to win a £1.5 million budget to develop the first phase of your European initiative. The internal business objective may be to win the support of at least 60 per cent of the main board for this initiative, before the budget meeting next month. Now you have a clearer sense of target. With 20 directors, 12 have to be identified and persuaded. You can segment the audience and begin to lobby those most likely to support the European strategy. Alternatively, you may be seeking the support for a new marketing plan from an operational team, giving the following objective:

- to have won support for next year's marketing plan and communicated its implications to all groups directly or indirectly involved in its implementation within two weeks.

Segmentation
The key here is not to treat all internal customers the same. Just like an external market, the audience requires segmenting, and a different approach may be required for each key group. Some segments may not be worth targeting. For example, a group of directors positively anti-Europe would be unlikely to be persuaded to support your pro-European strategy and so it would be better for you to split your audience into two:

- maintaining the support of those directors you know are basically European supporters
- concentrating your efforts on those who are waverers or undecided.

Within a team, different groups of workers may have various interests in the implications of this year's marketing plan. The bonuses of the sales team, the demands on the distribution team and the benchmarks imposed for improving customer care will need presenting differently to different teams.

Positioning

We have already indicated how a strategy could be positioned as high or low risk to influence senior managers, so change and plans can be presented in a number of ways to others in the company. In Fig. 10.6 changes or plans at position X may be attractive. It allows management to say, 'it is not our fault that change is needed', and adds the implied stick of what will happen if we do not change. The Y position is that taken by a management in control, optimistic, grabbing opportunities and forward-looking. The implied carrot in this approach is the excitement of change.

Fig 10.6 Positioning planning proposals

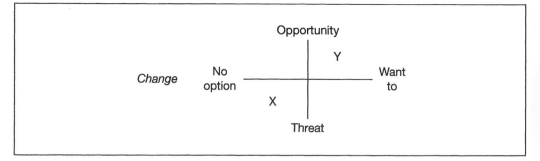

You can see how easy it is to apologize for plans and change, but if you position yourself at X it is very hard to motivate and be enthusiastic about the changes. If management comes across as unconvinced or unenthusiastic, then that message will quickly spread.

Managers need to give careful thought to how best to position their plan and then all messages related to it should be co-ordinated and internally consistent with it. There are many possible dimensions against which a plan could be positioned:

- high risk/low risk
- opportunity/threat
- short term/long term
- with little direct impact on staff/considerable impact on staff
- no option/choose to change
- easy to achieve/hard to achieve
- increase staff empowerment/reduce staff influence
- higher earning potential/lower earning potential
- make staff's jobs easier/makes staff's jobs harder.

You need to consider or change the plan you want to implement and the characteristics of your staff or other stakeholders before deciding on an appropriate positioning.

!!!

- Remember that, as with your external customers, it is important to build and retain a relationship with your staff. It is expensive to win new customers and equally expensive to recruit and train new staff. Long-term relationships depend on open communication channels but also on honest and reliable messages being transmitted.
- It is easy to raise expectations and then fail to deliver them, causing long-term dissatisfaction. If you win staff support for a proposal on the basis that it will be easy to achieve and have little direct impact on them and then proceed to make 10 per cent of the team redundant, your internal audience will not trust future messages.

Targeting

Within your identified market segments there will be key individuals whose support is essential. Your research should have identified these people so that a differentiated, probably personalized, approach can be made to them. These key influences are the equivalent of the early adopters in the purchase of any product or service – others will follow their lead. Your success depends on their enthusiasm for your plan.

!!!
- Do not assume that key figures are necessarily the formal team leaders or managers.
- Often they are informal social leaders, a trade union representative, the elder statesman of the factory floor, the reception staff who have contacts across the organization or most successful salesperson. You need to know the internal influences in your own business unit.

Internal marketing tactics

The 4Ps of the traditional marketing mix provide a framework for thinking through the implementation of an internal marketing plan.

The plan equals the product

What is the key change, idea or proposal that you are trying to win support for? Remember that features of the plan must be translated into benefits. For example, introducing a telesales team to support the field sales force could be presented to the sales team as an opportunity to increase effective sales time and so raise commission earned.

Recognize that what you are selling internally is the result of your external marketing plan, but it is not the same thing. For example, the decision to reposition your range as premium-priced and more exclusive could involve a number of internal changes, including:

- a reduction in the sales team's freedom to negotiate on price
- a change in selected distribution agents

- a new promotional image and communication style with customers
- possibly staff cuts if volume falls with the repositioning.

It is this recognition of the implications of a plan that is critical to implementation.

Place – when and where?
In marketing, 'place' is about the opportunity to purchase. In internal marketing, it is less obvious, but think of it in terms of when and where plans are made available for staff to buy into.

Timing can be critical – who gets told first and where. Major changes announced first at the annual sales conference are unlikely to be well received. Individual concerns cannot be voiced and there is opportunity for dissenters to band together. Even if you work with just a few people, selecting the right time and place to present proposals to them is a difficult decision.

Checklist
Consider the following when selling plans internally:

- choose times when staff are able to concentrate – i.e. not five to five on Friday or when they are rushing to meet a client
- work with smaller interactive groups to allow instant feedback
- delegate the task of disseminating information to others so that large numbers of staff can get the message at the same time
- choose a suitable venue, giving staff an environment in which they are comfortable to make comments and ask questions
- make sure briefings are undertaken in a way which makes those involved feel that their views matter, their support is essential and their contribution is valued. A 'take it or leave it' approach will do little to help you implement your plan successfully.

Price – what is the cost to me?

Price is another element of the mix that people sometimes have problems with when looking at internal marketing. There is of course seldom a price tag attached to any issue of change, but there is still a price to pay. Managers who recognize this and are able to build this into their internal plans will show considerable empathy with their audience.

Changes that may seem minor to you can be significant to the staff. Altering opening times from 9 a.m. to 8 a.m. may involve staff in problems of childcare and transport to school. Marginal changes to sales areas can increase travelling times or the number of nights spent away from home. It is your responsibility to recognize the price of your plan and be able to present benefits that make supporting the plan worthwhile.

Promotion – the message

In the internal market, promotion or communication works in much the same way as it does externally.

One-way broadcast messages act like advertising, allowing no opportunity for response. They create awareness and interest, but little attitude or behaviour change. One to one meetings or group briefings are like the personal sales effort and are more effective at changing behaviour but are very expensive in terms of management time.

As with an external market, a mix of communication techniques is best used, with staff briefings supported by reports, memos, appraisals and where necessary, training. Poster campaigns can be used to reinforce customer care, quality or health and safety plans, and staff newsletters and magazines are further useful channels in larger companies.

Communication plans should be built around quantified objectives related to your identified segments and targets; in this way internal communication will be focused and purposeful.

The most common complaint staff make of their managers is that 'they won't listen'. Make sure your internal communication plans incorporate mechanisms for feedback.

Controls

Constant review of how your plan is being accepted internally is very important. Staff attitude surveys, customer feedback and sales records are some of the mechanisms for monitoring the uptake of plans internally.

Some changes are relatively easy to monitor, such as the number of staff who have completed the customer care course. Others can only be judged against benchmarks established at the start of the process.

- Where possible identify tangible goals to help implement change. For example, a customer orientation can be complemented by achieving a quality standard like BS 5750, ISO 9000, or Investors in People.
- Setting an internal goal of achieving one of the above gives staff a real framework for change, which will help refocus the operation around the needs of customers.

A note on budgets

Internal marketing budgets may not be as extensive as external ones, but internal marketing does not come free. Management time must be found, and if changes require staff moves or training the bill for implementation can be significant and needs to be calculated into the overall cost of the proposal.

Controlling plans

If you have no intention of monitoring the progress of your plan during its implementation then there is very little point in producing the plan in the first place. Simply committing a plan to paper is not enough to make the desired outcome a sure-fire certainty. Control is not an option but an integral part of the planning process. Controls exist to close the planning loop, providing feedback on progress, effectiveness and informing next year's plans. Even small companies can easily build controls into their planning calendar and make it a routine element of all management activity.

Why controls are needed

Your plan was developed on the basis of a forecast of future events and activities within the external environment. Simply because eight months ago you assumed that your competitors would remain the same, is not an excuse to allow you to ignore the surprise launch of a new competitive product on the market. Economic performance may have proved different than was expected, the weather may have been unseasonably good or bad, or you may have underestimated the speed at which a new technology would be made available.

The longer the planning horizon the more likely that your forecasts will be wrong. Inaccurate forecasts are *not* a sign of bad management. Only when managers fail to recognize the variance between planned and actual events, and so fail to make appropriate changes to their plans, can they be described as poor managers.

Contingency planning and scenario plans go some way to preparing the business and the manager for the unexpected, but rapid feedback and early warning systems from the marketplace are critical if the manager is to have the opportunity to implement them. Your plan plays the role of a benchmark against which you measure your performance and adapt your strategy as needed in order to achieve your desired goal – see Fig. 10.7.

Plans should *never* be written in tablets of stone. They and the systems that support them need to be flexible and responsive. Deviations both higher and lower than forecast performance levels need to be responded to. If sales of product A were forecast at 104,000 units for the year and the first three months showed sales running not at 2,000 units a week but 3,000, that is not necessarily a cause for celebration and complacency. Marketing needs to revise its forecast. This may mean identifying why the forecast was wrong.

Fig 10.7 The indirect route to achieving your goals

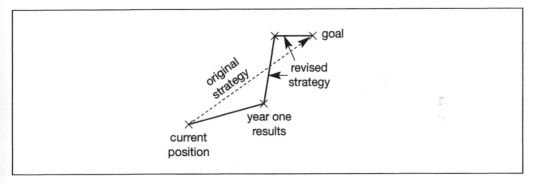

Turning defence into attack

Imagine the case of a football manager whose team only needs a draw to ensure its place in the final. His match strategy is a defensive one, but in the first 15 minutes the opposition score two unexpected goals. The defensive strategy must now be modified in favour of an attacking one which might level the scores and ensure the necessary draw. If the team simply redoubled its efforts at the old defensive strategy it might keep the opposition from scoring more goals but would fail to achieve the objective of a place in the final.

- Is the increase in demand temporary or likely to be permanent?
- What are the implications of this new forecast on production, distribution and finance?
- Are there adequate supplies of raw materials available, and can higher levels of demand for credit or after-sales service be satisfied?
- If available resources are diverted to servicing the higher demands for product A, what other products are not being serviced fully?
- What are the implications on profitability of this switch?

Cash-flow problems resulting from higher than forecast demand is a major cause of insolvency amongst smaller business. Do not make the mistake of ignoring those 'above forecast' results.

Successful managers recognize that it is the outcome that is important *not* the plan. The plan is simply a means to an end. Those who put the plan on a management pedestal, refusing to modify it or probably even refer to it from one planning cycle to the other, are those for whom planning is a barren activity, unlikely to yield the results desired.

- Build the expectation of modifying plans into your business calendar. Establish review meetings every two or three months with the agenda item, 'How do we need to change the plan?'
- If you and your management team begin to expect changes, the planning process will automatically become more dynamic and continuous.

The value of control

Planning is a cycle – see Fig. 10.8 – and the control elements close the loop, providing information valuable to the next

Fig 10.8 The planning cycle

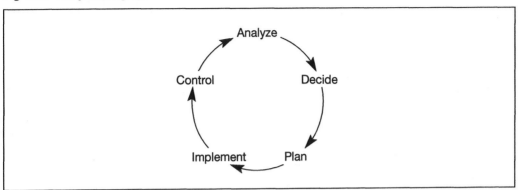

round of planning. Controls contribute to planning activities in three ways:

- they provide managers with warnings when actual performance is deviating from the forecast
- they provide input information into next year's planning activity
- they provide managers with information that allows them to evaluate their own planning competencies and so learn from planning experience.

An early warning system

Once plans have been based on specific and quantified objectives the basis for a simple system of control is clear. If you planned to sell 12,000 units in a year, at the end of a month you can check to see if you sold 1,000 or whether you are averaging 250 units a week.

However, this simple system may not take into account seasonal fluctuations in demand, so the manager needs to chart forecast sales over 12 months to get a true benchmark against which each month's performance can be judged – see Fig. 10.9.

Fig 10.9 Comparing actual and forecast sales

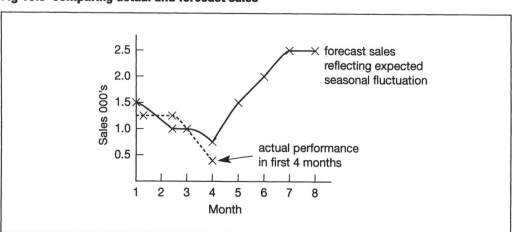

Instead of judging this month's performance with last month's, a process that fails to account for seasonality fluctuations, look at a moving annual total. Take the last 12-month total, then add the sales for month 13 and subtract those for month 1. Compare the total for the 12 months 2–13 with the original 1–12. If it is increasing, your performance is improving.

In Fig. 10.10 the annual sales total was 65 million units, generating a profit contribution of £1,300,000. If the results of month 13 are substituted for month 1 you can compare performance on an annual basis after taking account of seasonality fluctuations. The 12 months to the end of month 13 generated 64 million sales (total – month 1 + month 13) and generated £1,280,000 profit contribution – a decline in performance. If month 2 figures are now substituted by those for month 14

Fig 10.10

	Month 1	Month 2	Month 3	12-Month Total	Month 13	Month 14
Sales volume (M)	4	6	8	65	3	7
Profit contribution £ 000's	100	120	140	1, 300	80	130

then sales now equal 65 million (new total – month 2 + month 14) and profit contribution now equals £1,290,000.

To be of value, control information must be collected on a continuous basis, and its value is essentially related to its ability to identify trends. It is these trends that provide input to the analysis and forecasts of future plans.

In a real sense we have come full circle – information was the starting point for the planning activity, but it is also its finishing point. The quality of the organization's management and marketing information system is fundamental to its control activities. Sadly, it is smaller businesses that are least well equipped to withstand sudden changes and so often they have virtually no control mechanisms in place.

However, as we discussed in an earlier chapter, the information explosion many organizations are experiencing is only the tip of the iceberg. Better and faster information systems allow sales, stock levels and performance to be monitored on an hourly basis rather than a monthly one. Improved information tools should mean better control, if used effectively.

Avoiding overload

Managers need to identify clearly what information they need for effective control and then call for it, rather than being passive recipients of information. There is probably little point in monitoring sales hourly or even daily if reordering takes place weekly. Simply because it is possible to run a control does not necessarily mean it is a good use of management time to do it.

Exception reporting

One technique of control that can help reduce overload is exception reporting. With this technique, managers can see at a glance which of their products, outlets or staff are performing outside their budgeted or forecast activity. By adding to this model a 'margin of error', for example 4 per cent above or below the forecast level of activity, it is possible to see which centres are 'exceptional' and require immediate management attention.

Look at the information in Fig. 10.11 on a sales team: its performance against forecast sales revenue and sales calls.

The performances of sales staff A–P have been plotted on the grid and nine staff show up outside the area of 1–4 per cent above or below budgeted activity:

Fig 10.11 Exception reporting

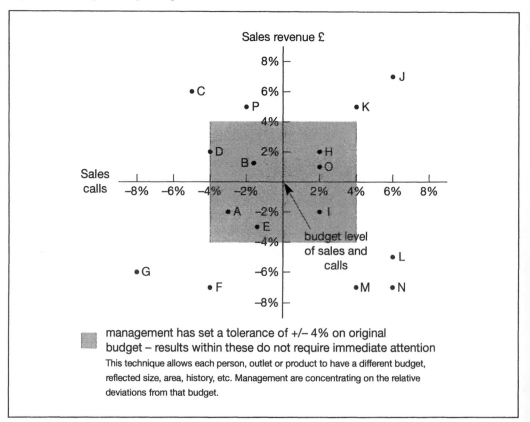

management has set a tolerance of +/– 4% on original budget – results within these do not require immediate attention

This technique allows each person, outlet or product to have a different budget, reflected size, area, history, etc. Management are concentrating on the relative deviations from that budget.

- C and P with sales revenue up and sales calls down
- K and J with sales calls and revenue up
- M, L and N with sales calls up and revenue down
- G and F with sales calls and revenue down.

The sales management team can now review these individual performances. M, L and N are a priority – sales calls and presumably expenses are up, but revenue is down. Perhaps they are not spending enough time with each client, are not qualifying their sales leads properly or need further sales training. They could perhaps benefit from working with C and P. Certainly, analysis of C and P's approach is important to cascade best practice to the rest of the organization.

Exception reporting maps also provide a useful basis for benchmarking. This year's position on the grid compared to last year's can give you a useful basis for comparison, between agents and over time.

!!!

- Do not jump too quickly to conclusions about the abilities of M, L and N, and G and F. There are two possible causes of their performance:
  - external factors peculiar to their sales areas – for example, regional recession and strong localized competition.
  - the original budgets were incorrectly set – for example, G and F may have been given the same sales call targets as K and J. If K and J are located in a city, increasing sales calls may be easy, but in G and F's rural areas the sheer physical limitations make the target impossible.
- Management should not make the mistake of using a control like exception reporting as a sole basis for performance appraisal. It does, however, flag up possible problem areas and provide a basis for prioritizing management attention and for further analysis.

Monitoring performance

Establishing the criteria by which performance is to be evaluated is a fundamental management responsibility – it should be addressed at the beginning of the planning process. Performance ratios, like those we discussed under the audit activities, are very useful for monitoring performance. Ratios enable you to benchmark performance across different parts of the business, across teams within the business, or over time across companies within a sector. Once trends have been highlighted that indicate a weakness in performance, management can investigate the causes and take corrective action.

The control process is essentially a simple one – see Fig. 10.12.

Fig 10.12 The control process

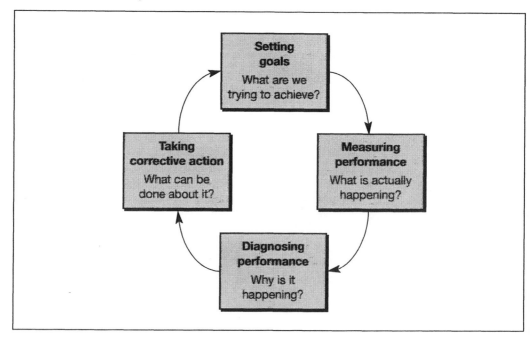

The diagnosis process is the dimension that provides managers with a greater insight into the behaviour of the market and the way in which marketing activities influence behaviour.

- Managers need to be careful when monitoring performance against set objectives. If the objective was too ambitious for the circumstances, or too conservative, then the actual performance can be misleading.
- Benchmarking against others in the industry is one approach, but care needs to be taken in determining which measures are most appropriate.
- The average of company performance in the sector or the market leader may well be misleading. Companies of whatever size need to identify close competitors – those of a similar size and characteristics provide more helpful and meaningful benchmarks.

A marketing performance checklist

Each manager needs to devise his or her own checklist, but it is likely to include measures to indicate the following:

- total sales volume and revenue, broken down by products and customers
- profitability of products and customers
- measures of awareness, attitude and action
- sales force and communication performance – for example, enquiries: sales; sales costs; average order values; and repeat purchase rates
- total sales and marketing costs
- market share performance
- profit performance of other industry players.

Measuring performance over time

The plan is dynamic, it takes place over time. The tactical action plans will have detailed what has to be done by whom. These can now be co-ordinated to produce a dated sequence of events. This can be usefully presented as a Gantt chart, against which the plan's implementation can be monitored and assessed.

A tactical plan for the staging of an exhibition may look like the example in Fig. 10.13.

Fig 10.13 Exhibition tactical plan

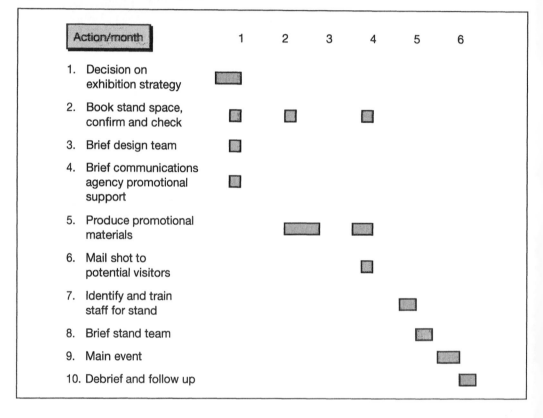

Action/month	1	2	3	4	5	6
1. Decision on exhibition strategy	▪					
2. Book stand space, confirm and check	▪	▪		▪		
3. Brief design team	▪					
4. Brief communications agency promotional support	▪					
5. Produce promotional materials		▪		▪		
6. Mail shot to potential visitors				▪		
7. Identify and train staff for stand					▪	
8. Brief stand team					▪	
9. Main event						▪
10. Debrief and follow up						▪

- When planning a sequence of events leave time for contingencies.
- Anticipate the unexpected and build in time for reprinting a piece of promotional material or briefing extra staff because of sickness.

Producing the timetable has another advantage in that it forces the team to consider the appropriate sequence of events, and means that individuals have a clear picture of the steps that must be taken and by whom – an excellent mechanism for internal communication. It is this detailed process that is the key to moving from planning as a theoretical exercise to a practical activity, intended to influence events. An effective plan needs a timetable just like a recipe needs its method. It is not enough to have the right ingredients for your soufflé; you must combine them in the correct sequence over time for the desired result.

The budget

The final element of control is the budget. This is simply the resources needed to implement the plan, expressed in financial terms. The budget is important, but its traditional role in top-down planning also causes problems – in the past it has often been used relatively inflexibly as a tool of financial control.

Departments are used to being allocated a budget and expected to get on with it – achieving whatever they could. The customer-oriented two-way planning approach is different because objectives are set that cascade down the organization. Each team in the hierarchy is asked to determine a strategy of how best to deliver that objective. Their plans are costed and collectively represent the necessary budget for that plan. This should not be unrealistic in terms of the organization's resources because it was only after a thorough audit of the available resources that the plan would have been devised.

This is an extension of the objective and task approach to budget setting described in chapter 9. It is another example of how senior managers must change if plans and organizations are to become customer-facing. Companies that in the

- Whilst managers need to ask 'what do you need to achieve X?' they can query the answer.
- Reviewing proposals to look for inefficiencies is quite acceptable and all staff should be encouraged to look for better ways of getting the same result, particularly at tactical level.

past have set budgets on the basis of an equal division of available resources between teams, or a formula based on 'last year's plus a bit', need to reconsider their approach. They should allocate resources to those sections or departments that most successfully marketed their plans to the resource holders.

Once the necessary budget has been calculated there is a final chance for the team to check the bottom line of its strategy by comparing the value of the outcome if objectives are achieved with the projected costs of achieving them. Two questions can usefully be applied:

- Do the proposition and plan look profitable?
- Could those same resources be used more effectively elsewhere?

Financial controls are essential to ensure that resources are then used as planned and to keep projects and teams within their budget. Cost control is as key to financial health and security as maintaining good customer relations, and all staff should understand the financial implications of their actions. Financial awareness should not be reserved for senior managers only.

Too many staff confuse revenue with contribution. They see the selling price and forget that only a fraction of it is available to cover costs. Vendors selling lottery tickets, for example, receive a margin of just 5 per cent. A wasted pound or dollar means 20 additional sales must be made to make up the loss. To the employee, economy measures can seem mean if the real finances of the operation are not understood.

Setting budgets can also contribute to this financial awareness. It is easy for staff involved in marketing activity to see only the marginal or direct costs of their efforts – a mailshot, for instance, based on the 50p cost of the brochure without any consideration for postage and administration. A more rigorous budgeting approach encourages a more realistic assessment and will help staff be more responsible for the resources they use.

> **!!!** Remember that if changed circumstances require plans to be modified, it is likely there will be budget implications that you must remember to think through.

Closing the loop

And so, as the plan is implemented over time a stream of data is generated on performance and effectiveness, which feeds into the management information system. This data can be called upon to inform future plans and to support next year's strategies and advise tactical planning.

The loop is part of a continuous process. The planning cycle acts as the wheel propelling the business forward – if it stops, the momentum will stop. If planning is haphazard, so commercial performance will be equally haphazard.

Planning must be more than just one of management's activities. It must be the central function and rationale for the management's role. Whatever the size of the business, the nature of the sector or the geographical location of the business, planning is a universal activity. We must take it seriously but demystify the process. Planning must be routine not special; informal and implemented rather than formal and reserved for the management elite. Perhaps most importantly, our plans must reflect our customer-facing philosophy – devised to satisfy customer and shareholder needs by ensuring resources are used both efficiently and effectively. Get planning right and any organization can get more from less.

---

nb

- Involve others as much as possible – the planning process and plans need to be shared.
- Base decisions on real customer feedback and research, not on hunch and experience.
- Invest in an information system developed to aid decision-making.
- Start with a clear picture of the strengths and weaknesses of the business and set realistic quantified objectives that take account of the relevant external environment.
- Be open-minded when identifying and evaluating strategic options, but once decisions have been made communicate them clearly.
- Only try to plan at SBU level and always produce a marketing plan for each product/market strategy being pursued.
- Translate business objectives so that those implementing the plans appreciate their implications.
- Make certain that marketing strategies are based around segment profiles that have some relevance or commonality in buying behaviour or motivation.
- Use positioning to co-ordinate and harmonize tactical activities to ensure synergy of effort.
- Build controls into plans from the beginning of the process.
- Use benchmarks that provide genuine insight into effectiveness and efficiency.
- Make planning a dynamic and ongoing process – remove it from its management pedestal and work with plans, and modify, change and adapt them as needed.
- Concentrate on implementation and use timetables and action plans to help in the shift from thinking to doing.

Index

action, 192
Ansoff Matrix, 39, 124
audit, functional, 34

Boston Matrix, 79–80
budget controls, 45, 255–257

change, implications of, 17
communication process, 204–207
communication tools, using the, 211–222
   advertising, 212
   direct mail, 221–222
   exhibitions and displays, 220–221
   merchandising, 221
   personal selling, 213–214
   point of sale, 221
   public relations, 218–219
   sales promotions, 214–217
competition,
   competitive activity, influences on,
      120–121
   competitor strategy, 117
   head-to-head, 118–120
   increased, result of, 6
   intelligence gathering, 116–117
corporate mission and vision, 132–133
   communicating the strategy, 144–145
   mission statement checklist, 134
   vision, 134
corporate objectives,
   content of, 135–136
   establishing, 41

culture change, 17–20
customer,
   analysis, 90–93
   expert, as, 6
   motivation of, 94
   planning focused on, 24
   profitability of, 96, 97, 99
customer orientation, 11–14
   building relationships, 22
   implementing a culture of, 25
   introducing, 21
   market research, 12
   pitfalls of, 13
   pro-active management, 23–24
   result of, 11

data or information, 58
decision-making, 207–209
deregulation,
   driving force of, 13
distribution, analyzing, 100, 103
diverse influences, 38

e-mail, making the most of, 58
environmental audit, 37
   analysis result of, 39
   census information, 112
   competition, 116
   head to head, avoiding, 118–120
   contingency plans, 122
   factors to be measured, 112–113
   intelligence, gathering, 111, 116
   international markets, 115

monitoring, 115
role of, 110
scenario plans, 122
significance of, 110
using an, 123–129

feedback, 46
functional audits, 34

GE Matrix, 82–88
comparing advantages, 88
competitive advantage, 87
customer criteria, 87
product attractiveness, 85
plotting, 89
product scoring, 86
relative attractiveness of options, 86
using, 84

information, assess, needs, 59
collecting to inform future plans, 257
data or, 58
decision-making, as aid to, 62
disseminating, 62
improving, 69
management system, 58
managing the input of, 56
marketing, 59
needs, prioritizing, 64
obtaining the, 57
sourcing the, 60–62
value of, 56
internal orientation, 9

management,
focus of, understanding, 7
information system, 58
internal orientation, 9
operational orientation, 8
philosophy of, 16
pro-active not reactive, 24
product orientation, 8

sales orientation, 9–10,
pitfalls of, 11
manager,
expensive resource, as, 19
prime task of, 5
role of, 3
market segmentation, 157–160
business to business, 161–162
checklist, 164
choosing and evaluating, 162–163
differentiated marketing, 167
integrating the mix, 165
lifestyle, 160
market positioning of a segment, 164
tactics of the marketing mix, 170
targeting, 166
marketer, role of, 203
marketing,
audit, after, 43
background, 149
buyer's market, result of, 12
information system, 59
developing an effective, 59–63
internal, 236–243
manager, role of, 7
mix,
6Ps add value, 172
adding value, 173
extended service, 189
integrating the, 165
matching customer demands, 177
targeting, 171 et seq.
need for, 6
objectives, 44
relevant, 155
translating, 152–154
plan, 43, 133–149
price, limited role of, 174
seller's market, strategy in, 8–9
strategy, 45, 148
determining, 156

tactics, 52
targeting, 166
marketing activity,
  assessing, 75
  auditing the, 72
  Boston Matrix, 79–82
  definition of, 73
  inputs to, 73
  outputs, 75–76
  product life cycle, 77–78
marketing planning,
  strategic, 118
marketing staff,
  qualities of, 74
market research, 12
  agency, selecting an, 66–67
  basics of, 65–66
  brief, the, 67
  information, review of, 68
  managing, 63–70
  portfolio analysis, 76–77
multi-factor portfolio model, 82

operational orientation, 9
organization,
  audit checklist, 101–102
  definition of, 3
  free flowing structure, 19
  pitfalls of expansion, 6
  traditional structures of, 18

Pareto Principle, 97
people, 190
performance,
  analyzing, 102–105
  measuring, 253–255
  monitoring, 252–253
  summary, 106–107
physical evidence, 191
place, 188–189
planning,
  activity, as an, 51–52

controls, 52
objectives, 51
strategy, 52
tactics, 52
challenge, a, 53
customer focused, 2
establishing a sequence, 30
gap, 42
  completing the, 137
  establishing, 137–140
  filling the, 42–43, 140–144
manager's role, 3
problems with, 30
rationale for, 2
review of, 26–29
sequence, reviewing, 47
tactical, 194
time, allocation of, 49, 50
timetable, 47–48
plans,
  controlling, 244–251
    avoiding overload, 249
    early warning system, 247–249
    exception reporting, 249–251
    need for, 244–246
    value of, 246–247
  functional, 31
  future, 257
  hierarchy of, 31–32
  intention of, 33
  making, work, 228
  problems with, 30
  separate, 32
  sequence of, 34
  target of, 53
  time to, 49
  winning support, 229
Porter's five forces, 121
presentation of plans, 230–234
  internal marketing, 236–243
  making them work, 228
  motivating implementers, 235–236

winning support, 229
price, 179–186
   break-even analysis, 181
   calculating profit and loss, 183
   challenge of pricing, 180
   marginal pricing, 184
   price setting, art of, 185
   price/value curve, 182
   problem with, 180
   public services and, 186
processes, 192
product orientation, 9, 22–23
promotion,
   activity, 187, 210
   analysis, 104
   effectiveness, 105–106
   plan, 222–225
   planning, 202

relationship marketing, 22, 94

sales orientation, 9–11,
   pitfalls of, 11
situational analysis, 36
societal orientation, 14
stakeholders,
   meaning, 3

strengths and weaknesses,
   analysis of, 36–37
success, 15
supply,
   increased, effect of, 10

timetable for action, 45
total product concept, 96, 178–179
transformation,
   process of, 4

value chain analysis, 192
value for money, 171